EX LIBRIS

That God's Works Might Be Revealed
Stories of Saints, Sickness, and Disability

Charlotte Riggle

PARK END BOOKS

Greenville, Michigan 2025

That God's Works Might Be Revealed: Stories of Saints, Sickness, and Disability

Copyright © 2025, by Charlotte Riggle

Cover Artist Mary Sarchizian

Publisher's Cataloging-in-Publication Data

Names: Riggle, Charlotte, author.

Title: That God's Works Might Be Revealed: stories of saints, sickness, and disability / written by Charlotte Riggle; cover design by Mary Sarchizian

Description: Greenville [Michigan]: Park End Books, 2025.

Identifiers: ISBN: 978-1-953427-25-0 Subjects: Religion – Christianity – Saints & Sainthood, Religion – Christianity – Orthodox

ALL RIGHTS RESERVED

No part of this publication may be reproduced, stored in a retrieval system, or transmitted in any form or by any means, electronic, mechanical, photocopying, recording, scanning, or otherwise, except as permitted under Section 107 or 108 of the 1976 International Copyright Act, without the prior written permission of the publisher except in brief quotations embodied in critical articles and reviews.

www.ParkEndBooks.com

If you have ever felt excluded because of a
disability
(whether your own or someone else's)
this book is for you

Table of Contents

St. Luca Casali	10
St. Finian Lobhar	48
St. Hervé	54
St. Etheldreda	65
St. Cenydd of Wales	108
St. Pimen the Much-Ailing	121
St. Theodore of Tobolsk	136
St. Hermann of Reichenau	162
St. Gerald of Aurillac	178
St. Angadrisma of Beauvais	220
St. John the Little	261
St. Nicholas of Myra	299
St. Odilia of Alsace	309
St. Thorlak of Iceland	342

Foreword

As Jesus passed by, he saw a man which was blind from his birth. And his disciples asked him, saying, Master, who did sin, this man, or his parents, that he was born blind? Jesus answered, Neither hath this man sinned, nor his parents: but that the works of God should be made manifest in him.

-John 9:1-3

The short stories in this book explore disability and sickness in the lives of Christian saints. The saints themselves would not have used the word *disability* to describe their conditions, because *disability* as a category word for physical or sensory impairments is incredibly modern. They might have used the word *affliction*, which in the late Medieval period carried the sense of ongoing suffering, but which earlier signified an act of humility, of casting down pride.

In different times, people not only used different words, they also had different ideas about the causes of bodily afflictions, and therefore different ideas about how (or whether) to deal with them. It wasn't until the late 19th century and early 20th century that germ theory of disease took hold. Before that, it was accepted that sickness was caused by miasmas (bad air that carried tiny seeds that could cause illness) or by a disruption of the humors. Other bodily afflictions could be caused by injuries, childbirth, demonic possession, or the evil eye.

Or by God. Not as punishment, though. For much of Christian history, the health of the soul was far more important than the health of the body. Bodily afflictions were a gift of God's grace, protecting the afflicted ones from sin, allowing them to focus entirely on Christ, and bringing them to salvation. St. Porphyrios held this view, saying, "My illness is a special favour from God, who is inviting me to enter into the mystery of His love and to try to respond with His own grace." For St. Porphyrios, as for so many saints who had come before him, illness is a means to acquire the grace of God.

My stories of these grace-filled saints are neither biography nor hagiography. Rather, they are historical fiction. I took what is known about the saint, dug into the discrepancies in the source materials, and then filled in the blanks to create a story. In this, the stories are rather like family stories, the kind of stories that we tell around the holiday table about our grandparents and great-grandparents. As these stories are passed down from generation to generation, details may be added, lost, or changed. I have embraced this tradition, holding tight to the details that I can confirm, and inventing whatever details or characters are needed to make the story work.

I have included bits of historical background that may be of interest to some readers in the notes at the end of the book, along with brief traditional prayers to the saints whose stories I tell.

St. Luca Casali
Born 8th century, Nicosia, Sicily
Died c 800, Agira, Sicily

FEAST DAY MARCH 2

On a beautiful summer morning, when the sky was a brilliant blue, as blue as Our Lord's robes in the apse at the church, Luca's mother told him that she was going to the market to buy dyestuff for her work. When he had gathered the eggs, made sure there was clean water for the chickens, and weeded the garden, he could go play with the village boys.

    Luca jumped up and hugged her.

    "Just stay out of trouble," she said, kissing his forehead and signing him with the cross.

    "I promise!" he said.

When Luca was done with his chores, he put a loaf of barley bread and a piece of hard cheese in a haversack and thought about what to do. He didn't much like playing with the boys in the village. He'd rather be in the woods alone. It was cool and quiet, like church. He thought about the cave deep in the forest, where snow from the mountains was stored for the tables of the kings and lords. If he were very lucky, there might be workers at the cave, who might offer him a handful of icy snow to eat with his bread and cheese.

He set off down the rocky path in front of his home. The path met up with a road, and the road wound its way around and down the steep hill. The air smelled of heat and dust and dry grass. He stopped to watch a moss-green lizard sunning itself on a rock. He reached out slowly, to touch it, but it darted away and disappeared.

Luca kept walking. He watched an eagle ride the air currents high into the sky, higher than the hills of Nicosia. At the crossroads, he turned north, out of the valley, towards the forest. The land was greener here. He wasn't yet in the forest, but there were trees. Not the scrubby trees that grew between the rocks beneath the eagle, but proper trees, straight and tall, trees that gave shade and shelter to everyone who passed them by.

He reached the spring that bubbled out between rocks beside the road. Two years ago, when he was young, his father showed him the spring. He was older now, and his father was gone. He scooped clear, cold water in his hands and drank. When he had enough, he rubbed his wet hands on his face, crossed himself, said a prayer for his father, then set out walking again.

The trees grew closer together here. Soon, they formed an arch over the road, and he was in the forest. The air was cool, filled with the sounds of birds twittering and chirping and calling to each other. Everything smelled of leaf mold and ancient trees.

In the forest, his steps didn't kick up puffs of dust as he walked. He jumped up and down, just to be sure, then spread out his arms and ran down the road like an eagle. His mother said if you loved God, you could run and never faint. So he ran until he couldn't run any more. He had a stitch in his side, and his chest was heaving. He sat on a rock to catch his breath and let the pain go away.

When he was ready to go on, he stood on top of the rock and looked all around. There was another rock ahead of him, and beyond that, the trunk of a tree that had fallen across the road. It was a recent fall; someone had taken an axe to it and opened the roadway, but no one had yet claimed the rest of the trunk for firewood. He jumped to the rock and then to the tree. There, he steadied himself and eyed a boulder ahead of him. If he swung his arms just so, and leaped as far as he could, he would, just maybe, land on top of it, like the king of the hill. If he missed, there was a deep blanket of leaf mold on the ground. It wouldn't hurt much if he fell.

He swung his arms, and leaped, and his feet caught the top of the boulder, then slid forward. He waved his arms wildly, trying to catch his balance. His felt his feet go up, and he felt the back of his head hit the rock, and then he didn't feel anything at all.

The bells on the bridles rang gently as Abbot Marco and his sister Maria rode up the forest road. Horses might have been better than mules for this trip. He'd have been higher up, and better able to see any dangers around them. Maria, though, had said that mules were more proper for an abbot and his sister. As always, she was right. They had come safe so far, by the grace of God and the protection of His Mother. They had not much farther to go.

Just ahead, something caught his eye. Something on the ground, near a large boulder. He pulled his mule to a stop. "Do you hear anything?" he asked Maria. She furrowed her brow, listening. "Nothing but wrens and blackcaps," she said, "and the wind sighing in the trees."

"I see something on the ground that I need to investigate," her brother said, "but I want to be sure it's not a trap. The bird songs could be brigands signaling each other."

They were both silent for a time. "I don't hear anything that sounds like people moving, or even a large animal," Maria said. "I think it's perfectly safe for you to investigate whatever it is that you see."

Abbot Marco dismounted from his mule, handed Maria his reins, and walked toward the boulder. "Why, I believe it is a child!" he exclaimed. He knelt and touched the child's face. It was warm. "Thanks be to God, he's alive."

"Was there any doubt?" asked Maria.

"He seems to have fallen," Abbot Marco replied. "It looks like he hit his head in his fall." He walked back to his mule and got his water skin. "I'll see if I can rouse him," he said.

"Do you need my help?" Maria asked.

"Not yet," Abbot Marco replied. He poured water from the skin into his hand and splashed the child's face. The child stirred. "My child," said Abbot Marco. "My child, speak to me." The child opened his eyes. "My child, can you speak?"

Luca thought someone was speaking, but he couldn't make out the words. He opened his eyes, and the world spun around, and the light stabbed his brain. He closed his eyes again, moaning softly.

"Here, take a sip of water," the man said, lifting Luca's head gently and putting the water skin to his lips. Luca took a sip and coughed. Coughing made his head hurt more.

"Can you move?" the man said. "Here, move your feet." Luca worked to make the words make sense. Feet. He moved his feet. "Now your hands. Can you move your hands?" Luca moved his hands. "Very good," the man said. "Can you tell me your name?"

Luca opened his eyes, to see where the voice was coming from, but the world was still spinning, so he closed them again.

"Child, do you have a name?"

Luca kept his eyes closed. His name. "Luca," he said.

"Well, God be praised, Luca. It looks as though you took a tumble off this great rock and hit your head. I am Marco, abbot of the

Monastery of St. Felipe in Agira, and the woman on the mule over there is my sister, Kyria Maria."

Luca opened his eyes again. The words were spinning away from him. He closed his eyes and the words came closer. "Am ... am I in trouble?"

"In trouble?" said Abbot Marco. "If we hadn't come along, you might well have been in trouble. It is dangerous to be injured and alone. But, no, you're not alone now, and we can tend to your injuries and look after you until we can return you to your family."

Luca didn't respond.

"Marco, the child's breathing is labored," said Maria. "He is in pain."

"Luca," said Abbot Marco, "Are you in pain?"

Luca nodded. Abbot Marco looked towards his sister. "The child nodded," he said.

"Luca, child," said Maria. "If you can tell us where your family dwells, we won't trouble you with any more questions."

"Nicosia," he said.

"God be praised!" said Abbot Marco. "We

are on our way to Nicosia. You must go with us, dear Luca."

Luca's eyes stayed closed.

"My brother, the child is in pain, and I believe he is exhausted. If you think it safe to move him, lift him up here and let him ride in front of me."

They rode slowly to Nicosia. Luca fell asleep leaning against Maria's chest.

"Luca," Maria said gently, "Luca, child, wake up." Luca stirred. "Luca, we are in Nicosia. My brother is going to lift you down from the mule and carry you inside."

"Nicosia?"

"Yes, we're at my home in Nicosia. It is at the foot of the hill of the Savior."

"Where's my mother?"

"As soon as we get you inside, you will tell me your mother's name, and I will send a servant to fetch her. Now, here, I'm going to slide you off my lap and into my brother's arms."

As Abbot Marco got Luca settled in his arms, Maria dismounted. "Where is my guide?"

she asked.

"Here, Kyria," said a tall, thin girl. Maria put her hand on the girl's shoulder, and they walked together through the entry hall and into the atrium of Maria's home.

Abbot Marco had settled Luca on a couch in the atrium and tucked him under a fur, then pulled a chair up next to him. "Now, who are your parents?" he asked.

Luca searched for the words to answer. "My father. Angelo. Died in the plague."

"May God grant him rest with the saints," said Abbot Marco. "And your mother, my child? Is she...?"

"Agata."

"Where is your home?"

"Archangel Michael," Luca said. "Near the top."

"Near the top of the hill of the Archangel Michael?" Abbot Marco asked. Luca nodded. "That's not far," the abbot said. "Kyria Maria's servant will find her and bring her here."

A servant appeared, holding a cup. He

stood silently until Abbot Marco turned to him. "Kyria Maria said the child is to have this," he said.

Abbot Marco took the cup. "My child, do you think you can hold the cup yourself? Or should I hold it for you?"

Luca looked at his hands. "I can hold it," he said. He took the cup. "What is it?"

"I believe it's willow bark tea," said Abbot Marco. "It may have poppy tears in it as well, and honey."

Luca sniffed the cup.

"My sister has some skill with herbs," said the abbot. "The tea may not be pleasant to drink, but it will help relieve the pain in your head."

Luca sipped the warm tea. It was sweet and woody and a little bitter.

"Drink it all," Abbot Marco said.

Luca drank, then laid back against the cushions. "I thought a man lived here," he said.

"Yes, you're right," said Abbot Marco. "The man who lived here is our nephew. His wife died in childbirth in the spring, and rather than take a new wife, he decided to join me at the monastery. He offered his house to his aunt, my sister. She lost her husband in the plague, just as your mother did. She was no longer happy in Cefalu, so she has moved here, to Nicosia."

Luca nodded and looked around. The room they were in was larger than his entire house, and there were doorways along every wall. He wanted to ask where the doors went, and why there was a window in the ceiling and a pool of water below it, and when his mother would get there, but his head still hurt, and he couldn't find the words.

"My sister is hoping that other widows of good character will join her here. They would live together in prayer and piety and works of mercy."

"My mother," said Luca. "My mother is a widow of good character."

"I'm sure she is," said Maria from a doorway behind them. "I'm also sure that my brother has been chattering with you far too long. When he's at the monastery, he keeps silence. When he's with me, he chatters like a squirrel. He needs to keep silence for a bit, so you can rest."

Abbot Marco sighed. "You are right, my

sister," he said, standing up. "Why don't you sit here with Luca, and I'll walk through the house and make sure everything is in order." Maria took his elbow, and he led her to the chair.

Luca wasn't sure if he had slept or not. He opened his eyes. The world didn't spin, and his head hurt only a little. Maria was still sitting with him. "Kyria Maria?" he said.

"Oh, child, you're awake! How is your pain?"

"It is better," he said.

"Thanks be to God," said Maria.

There was a long silence, as Luca looked around the room. The walls between the doorways were covered with paintings of a garden filled with flowers and birds. A river flowed between two of the doorways. Tall birds waded in the river, white birds, and pink, birds he had never seen before.

"Kyria Maria, may I ask you a question?"

"Of course, child."

Luca thought for a moment. He wanted to know about the tall birds, but there was another question that insisted on being asked first.

"Kyria Maria, promise I won't be in trouble?"

"No, child, you won't be in trouble."

"Kyria Maria, are you blind?"

"Yes, child, I am. I have been since I was a young child."

Luca nodded to himself and was silent a long while, looking at the birds. "May I ask you another question?" he asked.

"You may."

"Did God make me fall in the forest?"

"Do you think He made you fall?"

"I don't know," said Luca. The memories seemed to float away from him. He waited, and they floated back. "A long time ago," he said, "the priest got mad at me when I was jumping off the benches in church. He called me a knave, and he said that, since God hadn't punished me, he would do it. He had one of his servants take me out and beat me."

Maria furrowed her brow. "Why were you jumping in the church?"

An image floated into view. "In the church,

above the apse, there is an icon of a white bird on a throne. My mother told me the bird is God, Not God the Father, but God like the Lord Jesus is God, and I wanted to see it and kiss it." He sighed. "I know, if you love God enough, you can fly on wings like an eagle. My heart was all full of God's love, so I wanted to fly to the icon. I wanted to kiss God."

Maria and Luca were both silent, listening to their own thoughts and to the small birds that twittered in the courtyard. Finally, Luca spoke again. "Being in the forest sometimes feels like being in the church, Kyria Maria. Maybe God doesn't like people to jump in the forest, either, so maybe he was punishing me."

Maria considered the words of this unusual child. "I think, Luca," she said, "that the beating you got from the priest's servant was enough to cleanse a child's soul from the sin of being disorderly in the church."

Luca nodded. "That's what my mother told me. She also told me not to go into the church again, unless I had someone with me to keep me out of trouble."

Maria cocked her head to one side. Abbot Marco had stepped into the atrium. "Marco, my brother, do you think, between us, we could take this child to church and keep him out of trouble?"

Abbot Marco looked at his sister and the child. "I think we could," he said.

When Luca's mother arrived, she bent her knee to Abbot Marco and kissed his ring, then bent her knee to Kyria Maria. "Thank you for caring for Luca," she said. "I hope he has not been too much trouble. I will take him home now."

"Good mistress Agata, he has been no trouble at all," said Kyria Maria. "Supper is being prepared. My brother and I would be honored to have you and Luca join us at our table."

"I'm afraid I can't trouble you so much, Kyria," she said.

"If you will not accept a meal as a blessing," said Abbot Marco, "then accept it as penance if you must. The meal is ready."

Agata bowed her head. "Yes, my lord abbot," she said.

It was a simple supper: smoked fish, pickled octopus, bread, olives, and lentils. When those were cleared away, the servants brought figs and cheese. Luca fell asleep listening to the voices of the adults. As he slept, he dreamed. In the dream, his father and the abbot stood in the church. The God-bird was shining, and an angel flew down from the wall and talked to them and blessed them.

When he woke, the dream was gone. Lamps on the table created a pool of light in the darkness, and the adults were still talking.

As Luca had slept, Abbot Marco had begun to feel that the child's life was somehow tied up with his own. It was more than the simple fact that he and Maria had saved the child's life. He found himself telling Agata that, while he was in Nicosia, he wanted Luca to study with him, to learn reading and writing and the lives of the saints. Agata demurred, saying that after so many of her customers had died in the last plague, she had barely enough work to provide food and shelter for herself and her son. She could not pay for his education. Abbot Marco said that he would commission her to embroider new vestments for the clergy and altar of his monastery, the monastery of St. Felipe in Agira. That would pay for Luca's studies and anything else he might need.

Maria joined her words to her brother's. She told Agata that she needed a guide to walk with her to and from the church every morning. Would Agata consent to Luca going to church with her?

Agata consented, wondering at the change in her fortune.

That night, Luca and his mother slept in one of the chambers that opened from the atrium. A serving girl slept just outside the doorway in case they should need anything during the night.

When the sun rose, the serving girl brought a basin and pitcher so they could wash. Luca could hear Abbot Marco chanting prayers somewhere in the house, and servants singing as they worked. He sat up. He hadn't realized, when his mother carried him to the bedchamber the night before, that the river painted on the atrium wall flowed into the bedchamber. "Look, Mother!" he said. "Look at the birds! They're in the atrium too. What are they?"

His mother looked at the birds as she wiped her hands on the linen towel that the serving girl handed her. "I believe they are flamingos and egrets," she said. "Such birds live in the salt marshes by the ocean. Now stand and wash."

Luca stood and washed. As the girl took the bowl and basin away, Kyria Maria and Abbot Marco appeared in the doorway. "How is Luca?" asked Maria.

"He seems better this morning," Agata replied.

"Thanks be to God and the saints!" said Abbot Marco.

"He should rest today," said Maria. "My servants will take the two of you home on one of my mules. Tomorrow, Luca can come and walk with me to church."

The gate was open, so Luca walked through the narrow passage and into the atrium. A serving man was there, but Kyria Maria wasn't. Luca wasn't sure what to do, so he simply stood there silently.

The serving man looked him over. The child was dressed in a white woolen tunic that came to his knees. His face and hands were clean. His appearance would not embarrass the household. "Follow me," he said.

Luca followed him across the atrium and through a narrow passageway to the courtyard. As they entered, a dozen small birds flew up over the roof and away.

"Luca, you've frightened the chaffinches away!" said Maria.

"I'm sorry, Kyria Maria," said Luca. "I didn't mean to. Am I in trouble?"

"Of course not," Maria said. "The chaffinches love the courtyard, and they'll be back as soon as everyone here is still."

Luca sat as still as he could on a low stone wall, and he looked around. The courtyard was larger than the atrium, open to the sky. There were deep porches all around. Every space the sun could reach was filled with small trees, sweet smelling herbs, and flowering plants.

"Kyria Maria, can I ask you a question?"

"Yes, you may. You will not be in trouble."

Luca nodded, then remembered that he had to speak. "Thank you, Kyria Maria. How did you know the birds were chaffinches, since you can't see them? How did you know they flew away?"

"Luca, my child, I may be blind, but I am not deaf. I can tell one bird from another by its song, just as any sighted person can. I knew they flew because they stopped singing in the courtyard, and when they sang again, their voices came from beyond the roof." She stood up. "Now, Luca, let us go to church. You'll need to lead me there, of course. I don't yet know the way. Keep in mind that leading a blind person is nothing like leading a horse or a mule. You won't pull me or push me. You'll stand on my left side, just in front of me, and I'll put my hand on your shoulder. As you walk, I'll follow."

That day and the days that followed were peaceful and happy and good. Luca would kiss his mother in the morning and receive her blessing before walking down the path to Kyria Maria's home. He would greet Kyria Maria in the courtyard, then walk with her to church. After church, when they got back to her house, Abbot Marco and Luca would settle in the office, which opened to the atrium on one end and the courtyard on the other. There, Abbot Marco taught Luca to write and to read the Gospel, the Psalms, and the lives of the saints. After the day's lessons, they would chant the mid-day prayers, then have a meal of bread and cheese, along with a few olives or lupine seeds.

When they finished eating, Luca had lessons with Kyria Maria. On sunny days (and most days were sunny in Nicosia), they would walk in the courtyard or in the herb gardens behind the house, where she taught him to identify the plants and assess their virtues not just by sight but by smell and touch as well.

On rainy days, they would work together in Kyria Maria's workroom. She taught Luca to put the workroom tools, the knives and spoons, the mortars and pestles, the bins and crocks, in exactly the same place every time he used them. She taught him to sing the songs of healing, and once he knew the songs, she taught him how make remedies from herbs and resins they gathered from the gardens and how to preserve them and store them for future need.

After Luca left for the day, Kyria Maria had her own lessons. She and her brother would walk around the house, from one room to another. She learned the place of every door and window, every chair and chest, every statue, every candle and lamp. She studied the storerooms, so that she could inventory them independently.

Once she knew every inch of her home, Abbot Marco and Maria began studying the paths and roads in and around Nicosia. Their goal was for her to be as confident and independent here as she had been in Cefalu.

On the eve of the great feasts, Abbot Marco would take his mule and go back to his monastery in Agira so that he could celebrate the feasts with the brethren. Sometimes he took Luca with him. Luca would ride Kyria Maria's mule. He liked the way the bells on the mule's bridle jingled as they rode.

At the monastery, when the prior was giving Abbot Marco a report on all that had happened since his last visit, Luca would walk with one of the monks around the monastery grounds. "Keep the lad out of trouble," Abbot Marco would say with a wink.

These blessed times eventually came to an end. "My sister knows every street and shop in Nicosia now," Abbot Marco told Luca as they sat together in the courtyard, watching chaffinches and blackbirds flit among the trees and fountains. "She needs a guide only to make sure she doesn't trip over obstacles that ought not to be there, but she needs no one to tell her where she is, or what route to take to go where she wants to go. She no longer needs me here."

"But, my lord abbot!" said Luca. "I need you here!"

"You don't need me, my child. You have mastered your letters, and you know the lives of the saints as well as any child, and better than most adults. You're also very nearly as good with herbs as my sister, and that's no small thing. You have the knowledge and the means to live well and to care for yourself and your mother."

"But Abbot Marco! You can't go. If you leave, how will I become a monk?"

Abbot Marco looked at Luca curiously. "You want to become a monk? You have never mentioned this before."

"I thought you knew!" Luca said. "When we go to the monastery for the feasts, when the brothers are chanting the prayers in the chapel, their voices sound like rain and thunder and angels in the courts of heaven. I want to be there more than anything."

"There is more to being a monk than praying and singing, you know."

"I know," said Luca. "When you are with the prior, the brothers who walk with me tell me how they pray and work and study and do everything together, so that they can learn to love God."

"You don't have to be in a monastery to pray and work and study, my child. A monk must learn to love God through humility and obedience as well."

"I am obedient, Abbot Marco. You have said so yourself."

"I have said so, my son, that is true," Abbot Marco said. "You also have the humility that is natural for a child, for such you are. Yet I can't take you. Your mother needs you. She wouldn't be safe alone in the house on the hill."

"My mother is a widow of good character," Luca said. "She can stay here and pray and do good works with Kyria Maria."

"Even if that were possible, Luca, my child, you are too young to receive the tonsure."

"I can be an oblate now, and I can receive the tonsure when I'm old enough."

The abbot and the boy stared at each other. Finally, the abbot sighed and nodded. "I will talk to my sister, Luca, and to your mother. Perhaps it may be so."

It was the feast day of St. Luke the Evangelist when Abbot Marco and Luca set out for the Monastery of St. Felipe. Although it was Luca's name day, they didn't attend mass. They would be walking to the monastery, not riding as was their usual custom, so they had to get an early start. Abbot Marco's mule would be carrying his books and icons and the altar vestments that Agata had made.

As Abbot Marco supervised the loading of the mule, Luca walked through the house that he now thought of as his second home, bidding goodbye to the birds in the courtyard and the birds on the walls, the statues in the atrium and the servants in the kitchen. Then it was time for them to leave. Luca bowed to Kyria Maria, then hugged his mother tightly. "Just stay out of trouble," she said, kissing his forehead and signing him with the cross.

The road towards Agira was dry and dusty. The air was cool; the pale blue sky was streaked with thin, high clouds. Luca chattered happily as they walked, pointing out interesting looking plants and birds and speckled lizards sunning themselves on rocks.

Shortly after midday they stopped to eat.

Luca chose a flat rock to serve as their table, then pulled bread and cheese and figs from his pack. As they ate, Abbot Marco noted how far they had come and eyed the position of the sun in the sky. "Let's keep moving," he said.

By midafternoon, Luca was tired. "How much longer do we have to go?" he asked.

"I believe we'll get there around sundown," Abbot Marco said.

Luca didn't want to walk until sundown, but he knew he had no choice. He watched an eagle riding a current high above them. "I wish I could fly on wings like the eagles," he said.

"I'd be satisfied if I could simply walk and not be weary," Abbot Marco replied.

"Are you weary, too?"

"Of course I am."

Luca pondered the abbot's words as they walked. Their shadows were stretching long on the dusty road.

Luca adjusted quickly to life at the monastery. He was already used to filling his days with work, study, and prayer. In the winter, he assisted the infirmarer in preparing poultices, teas, and remedies for the monks who were ill. In the spring, he worked in the medicinal garden. He memorized the Psalms and the Gospels and all the services. When he was 12 years old, Abbot Marco and the brothers agreed that, although Luca was young, he was ready to take the monastic vows. Just a few years later, he was ordained to the priesthood. When the old infirmarer died, Father Luca was put in charge of the infirmary.

Then came the terrible winter. An illness swept through the monastery. It came with fever and fatigue, aching joints and an unrelenting cough.

Father Luca asked Abbot Marco's blessing to miss the times of prayer so that he could tend the sick. He made draughts of coriander and chamomile for the fevers, tea of willow bark and poppy tears for the aches, and a syrup of licorice, comfrey, and honey for the cough. If the syrup didn't subdue the cough, he made poultices of onion and applied them to the sufferer's chests.

For the younger monks, the active phase of the illness lasted at least a fortnight, if pneumonia didn't set in. As they recovered, those who had been ill needed at least another fortnight of convalescence to regain their strength. The old monks were sick longer, and many didn't survive. Father Luca couldn't take the time away from the living to attend the funerals for the departed. He hoped that they would understand.

One evening, Abbot Marco came to the infirmary. He was coughing. Father Luca put him to bed and brought him cough syrup and the draught for his fever. He told him frankly that he would be miserable for a time, but he would, by God's grace, recover.

In this, Father Luca was wrong. Abbot Marco's cough did not abate. He developed pneumonia. His skin was pale, his lips gray. He told Father Luca to call the brethren so he could give them his final blessing and receive their forgiveness.

"No, Abbot Marco!" said Father Luca, with tears in his eyes. "No. You can't die. If you die, who will be my father?"

"My son, my Luca," said the abbot, struggling to speak. "Truly, you don't need me anymore. You have the knowledge and the wisdom to care for yourself and your brothers."

Father Luca nodded, unable to speak. He summoned the brethren, those who were not ill.

They received Abbot Marco's blessing, and he received their forgiveness. Slowly his cough subsided, and he passed from this life into life everlasting.

After Abbot Marco died, the monks chose Father Luca to be their new abbot. In humility, he declined. They insisted. He refused. Finally they sent a delegation to the pope, asking him to command Father Luca to be the abbot. The delegation returned with a papal decree. The priest-monk Luca was now the abbot of the monastery of St. Felipe.

In the summer after the terrible winter, Abbot Luca noticed that he needed sunlight to read. By winter, he realized that candle flames and indeed anything that shone brightly looked smeared to him.

That spring, he understood that his eyesight was failing him, and that he would soon be blind. He decided that he would visit his mother and Kyria Maria one more time while he could still travel alone. When he returned to the monastery, he would resign his position as abbot, so they could elect someone capable of fulfilling the abbot's duties.

He set out for Nicosia after the Feast of the Resurrection, leaving the prior in charge.

"You've decided what, my lord abbot?" said Kyria Maria. Her voice was as sharp as the knives in her workroom.

Abbot Luca looked around the courtyard in silence for a moment. The air was filled with the smells of sunlight and spring. He could still see the grapevines draping the eaves of the porches, the tall spikes of echium, and the colors of borage, thyme, and poppies blooming in the beds. He could hear the songs of the women as they worked in the house, and the songs of the chaffinches in the garden as they flitted from the edge of the roof to the flowers and among the trees.

Finally, he spoke. "I've decided that, when I return to the monastery, I'll resign as abbot," he said again. "The brethren will elect a new abbot, one who can fulfill his duties."

"Why do you think you won't be able to fulfill your duties?"

"I told you, Kyria. I am losing my sight."

"I understand that, my lord abbot," she

said. "I fail to see how your failing eyesight has anything at all to do with your fulfilling your duties, and I will not help you share this sad news with your mother when she returns. Help me, saints of God! Did you learn nothing from me when you were a child?"

"I learned how to make remedies to ease suffering and cure illnesses, Kyria."

"My lord abbot, you learned more than herbs and remedies. In my workshop, you learned how to live with a blind person. You learned to put tools away in precisely the same place every single time. You learned to tell me when you came in the room and when you left. You learned not to move furniture about. You learned that better than my brother ever did. The monks at Agira can learn those skills as well."

"But, Kyria ..."

"Listen to me, Luca. You learned that a blind person can have knowledge and authority. Do I not manage this household? Do I not command the servants? Do I not tend this garden, choosing what to plant and where? Do I not harvest the herbs and store them and make remedies for my household and all the sick in Nicosia? Do I not pray? Do I not go where I please and do what I choose?"

"You do, Kyria."

"Am I not blind?"

"You are, Kyria."

"When you are blind, you will manage your monastery. You will command the brothers God has put in your charge. You will teach them to put things in precisely the same place every single time. You will work and pray and go where God sends you and do whatever else you choose to do. But you will not resign. Do you understand me? Or do I need to go see the pope myself, and tell him that you are stubborn and intransigent and afraid?"

"I am not afraid, Kyria."

"Do not lie to me, Luca," she said. "Do not lie to yourself, and do not lie to God. You—" She stopped. She had just called the abbot by his baptismal name, and she had called him a liar. She pressed her lips together so she couldn't say anything else. What else had she said? Finally, she spoke. "Forgive me, my lord abbot," she said. "It seems that I forgot that you are no longer a child, and I am no longer your teacher. The way I just addressed you is inexcusable. Forgive me."

"God forgives, Kyria Maria."

"And you?" she asked. "Do you forgive?"

"I forgive you with my whole heart, Kyria. Will you forgive me?"

"Forgive you? For what?"

"For lying to you, Kyria, and for lying to myself and to God. Because you are right. I am afraid."

Maria tipped her head and folded her arms. "You would be a strange man indeed if you were not afraid. You do not yet know enough about being blind to keep the fear away. But you will learn. I will teach you." Her voice softened. "God chose you to be the abbot of the monastery of St. Felipe after my brother, and you will be the abbot of the monastery of St. Felipe until God pleases to take you from this life. If it pleases God to take your sight, then you will be a blind abbot. But an abbot you will be."

Luca spent a month with Kyria Maria and his mother and the other widows who had joined them in the house. During the hours set aside for study, Kyria Maria taught Abbot Luca more of the things he would need to know to rule the monastery as a blind abbot.

When he returned to the monastery, he told the brethren that God had chosen to take his sight. It was imperative, therefore, that they learn how to live with a blind abbot before his sight was entirely gone. He assigned some of the brothers to read to him and to write for him. He assigned other brothers to walk with him. All of them, he commanded to put everything exactly, precisely where it belonged, so that he would be able to reach for anything he needed, even if he couldn't see it. He expected them to fulfill these obediences without fail.

In their love for their abbot and their love for God, in their mercy and obedience, the brethren did all that Abbot Luca commanded. Their skills and habits grew as Abbot Luca's sight failed, and by the time he had no sight left, he realized that he no longer had need of it.

From time to time, Abbot Luca made the trip to Nicosia to visit Kyria Maria's home, that he might learn from her and give spiritual counsel to the widows who lived there. He took two monks with him as servants and guides, and one of the oblates to give the child the joy of new places.

Early in the morning on the last day of one of these trips, while Abbot Luca was in the study sharing some final instructions with Kyria Maria and his mother, his companions rested in the courtyard. The monks talked in low voices as the oblate watched the birds that fluttered in the garden. The monks decided that, on the way back to Agira, they would play a prank on their blind abbot. They told the oblate that their lord abbot had a test for them, and they explained to him the part he would play.

The child, in his innocence, believed the monks. As they walked down the road towards Agira, he chattered happily, pointing out interesting looking plants and birds and moss-green lizards sunning themselves on rocks. When they were well away from Nicosia, the monks signaled to the boy that it was time for the test. He turned around. "Look, brothers!" he said. "There is a great crowd following us! It looks as though half the people of Nicosia are coming! Abbot Luca, they must want you to tell them again about the mercy of God."

Now, Luca was blind, but he wasn't deaf. He knew the calls of the birds, and the voices of people, and he could tell who entered a room by the sound of their steps. If there had been a crowd following them, he would have known. There was no crowd.

"My child," he said, then stopped. He was about to ask the child why he lied, then realized that the monks must be playing a prank. He decided to play along. "My child," he said, "find us a rock where you and I can sit and wait. As the crowd arrives, our brothers will direct them to sit on the ground, and I will teach them."

While they waited, Abbot Luca listened to the songs of the birds and the sighing of the wind. The monks began giving instructions to the people of Nicosia, the people who made no sound, who had no voices, who weren't there. The monks told the people to gather around Abbot Luca and sit on the ground. At last, one of the monks told Abbot Luca that all was ready.

"Which way will I find them?" asked the abbot, as he stood up from his rock.

"Turn just a little way towards the sun," said one of the monks. "There! You're facing them now."

"You can stand on the rock," said the oblate, "so they can all hear you better."

Abbot Luca smiled. "What a wise child you are!" he said. He stood up on the rock and preached a sermon to the trees and the rocks and the birds and the sky. It was a sermon for the ages, flowing with mercy and joy, with goodness and truth, with grace and peace. At the end of it, when Abbot Luca said, "In the name of the Father, and of the Son, and of the Holy Spirit" and made the sign of blessing, a thundering roar filled the air around them as the rocks shouted, "Amen!"

The monks fell to the ground before their abbot in fear. They confessed their deception and begged his forgiveness with tears. "Arise, my sons," Abbot Luca said. "I forgive, and God forgives." He kissed them each, and blessed them, and put his hand on the older monk's shoulder. "Now let us go. We have many hours yet to walk. May God give us strength for the journey."

St. Luca Casali

The source materials related to St. Luca Casali are exceedingly brief. They say nothing of St. Luca's parents, and they give the abbot of St. Felipe of Agira neither a name nor a sister. It seemed to me that the abbot needed a reason to live in Nicosia, away from his monastery, so when I gave him a name, I also gave him a sister. I made her blind, because I knew that St. Luca was going to lose his sight. When I was afraid that I might lose my sight, a friend who is blind told me that I had an advantage that most adults who lose their sight don't have. I have blind friends, and they would be able teach me how to function as a blind person. I wanted St. Luca to have that same advantage.

After St. Luca's death, a church dedicated to him was built at the place where the rocks had cried Amen.

Prayer
God honored you because of your obedience and exalted you because of your humility. Therefore we turn to you, O holy Abbot Luca: Intercede for us with Christ our God, that our souls may be saved.

St. Finian Lobhar

Born 6th or 7th century, Bregia, Leinster, Ireland
Died 6th or 7th century, Clonmore, Ireland

FEAST DAY MARCH 16

Once there was, or there was not – is anything certain but God's mercy? – a boy named Finian. Yet I will say that there was such a boy, because Finian was a common name for boys in Ireland.

Some say Finian was born here, and some say he was born there, and since there were many Finians, it seems that all these places are the true birthplace of Finian. Yet I will say that our Finian was born in Bregia, in Leinster.

Our Finian was a disciple of St. Columba, unless St. Columba had already died when Finian was born, in which case our Finian was a disciple of the disciples of Columba. Our Finian founded a church and a monastery at Innisfallen, unless that was Finian Cam. There is just so much we don't know.

Yet we do know that, by God's mercy, our Finian loved God with all his heart. When you love God as much as Finian loved God, that love fills your heart and dances like a fountain and flows like a river and soaks everyone who comes near it so that they are dripping with God's love and God's mercy, because love and mercy flow together.

When Finian traveled to the south of Ireland, to the land where his mother was from, the love and mercy that flowed from Finian healed the sick and raised the dead and reconciled enemies. The bishop there, seeing the love and the mercy that flowed from Finian, made him a bishop.

One day a woman brought her son to Finian. The boy was blind and deaf and leprous. Finian took the boy in his arms, and washed him with love and mercy and tears, and asked God to heal him. God said no. Finian asked again, and God told him that he would heal the boy if Finian would take the leprosy upon himself.

Finian said yes, and giving thanks to God for his love and his mercy, he handed the boy back to his mother. The boy was completely healed. Finian had leprosy.

A penitent asked Finian to make him a leper, too, so that by sharing this affliction with Finian, he might likewise be assured of salvation.

Finian refused. He told the man that he would not be able to bear the pain. When the man could not persuade Finian, he turned to

God. He asked God to give him leprosy, and God granted his request. The man endured as many hours or days as he had strength, then he returned to Finian and asked to be healed. Finian sent him to wash in a nearby pool of water, and as soon as the man washed, he was healed.

Finian served as a bishop for many years. When there was no food, he provided food. When there was no wine for the Eucharist, he blessed water, and it became wine. When a tree was barren, he blessed it to bear fruit. When a tree bore bitter fruit, he blessed it, and its fruit became sweet.

When he had suffered long and grown old and shared God's love and mercy and healing and hospitality to all who had need of it, a chariot descended from heaven to the place where he stood. In the chariot was a man who was old and beautiful, his hair as white as his linen tunic, his eyes as bright as the stars. With him was a woman who was wrapped in a shaggy cloak of reddish-brown wool shot with threads of silver, a rich-looking cloak that would keep a person dry and warm on a cold and rainy day. The world around the chariot seemed to become thin, like gauze, and even though the night was cold, the air was filled with the gentle hum of bees and the fragrance of wildflowers and honey.

"Who are you?" Finian asked.

"I am Brigid, the patroness of Ireland," said the woman.

The old man with Brigid said, "I am Maidoc, the servant of Christ," and his face shone with a light like that of the moon. "Tomorrow you and your people will celebrate my feast, and the day after you will celebrate the feast of this holy maiden, and she and I will bless all the places we love and all those who honor us. Then, dear Finian, beloved man, you will ascend with us to heaven."

Then the saints and their chariot disappeared, and Finian arose and went to Kildare and told the people there all that he had seen and heard. On the third day, Maidoc's promise was fulfilled, and Finian joined Maidoc and Brigid and all the saints in the land where there is neither sickness nor sorrow nor sighing, but life everlasting.

St. Finian Lobhar

There were perhaps a dozen Irish saints named Finian. It is and always has been hard to keep them all straight. The two you're most likely to encounter are Finian Lobhar and Finian Cam, the "squinty one," who may (or may not) have had a large hump on his back.

Lobhar means Leper. In St. Finian's time, the condition that we know as Hansen's disease did not exist in Ireland. Rather, the word leprosy was used for a wide range of chronic conditions affecting the skin.

In the early Medieval period, it was widely accepted that the poor man in the parable of Dives and Lazarus had leprosy. Based on this parable, many believed that those who had leprosy would go immediately to Heaven on their deaths. Rich people who wanted to escape the fate of Dives funded institutions for the care of people with leprosy. People from wealthy families who contracted leprosy were often cared for in their own homes.

After the Black Death appeared in Europe, attitudes towards leprosy began to change. Even so, it was never so bad as portrayed by the Victorians, who projected back on Medieval Christians the policies they were promulgating towards people with leprosy in the countries they had colonized.

St. Finian's feast has always been kept on March 16, even though his vision of St. Maidoc and St. Brigid puts the day of his death on February 2. It's possible that March 16 commemorates the translation of his relics, or the founding of a church consecrated to him, but as with so much about St. Finian, no one really knows.

Prayer
Lord God, Almighty Father, you gave St. Finian to be a minister for eternal salvation to your people. Grant, we beseech you, that we who had him on earth as a teacher may be worthy to have him as our advocate in heaven.

St. Hervé

Born around 521 in Guimiliau, Brittany, France
Died around 575, Lanhouarneau, Brittany, France

FEAST DAY JUNE 17

Winter had passed, and the sun again shone in the land of Brittany. Calves and lambs were in the fields, chickens scratched around the houses, birds sang in the forests, and farmers sowed their seed in hope. As the sun filled his heart with joy, the Welsh bard Hyvarnion set out from the court of Childebert I, King of the Franks, to visit his kinsmen in Wales.

As he made his way down the narrow forest road, he heard a voice of such transcendent beauty that he thought perhaps he had joined those who had died in the dark and cold of winter, and that he heard an angel singing. He pulled his horse to a stop and listened, hardly daring to breathe. Yet he breathed, so he must not be dead. Perhaps the voice was the elf queen? For surely no mortal ever had such a voice.

Hyvarnion couldn't tell where the voice came from. It seemed to fill the green wood, as if the oaks and hazels were themselves singing. Was it a tree spirit, then? He turned his head to better catch the notes. He thought perhaps the voice was ahead of him. He gave the horse a light squeeze with his legs, and the horse began walking slowly down the road.

When the voice stopped, Hyvarnion stopped. Had he frightened the creature away? But no, the voice came again, closer now. Hyvarnion's heart beat faster. A maiden pushed aside the hazel branches, ducked under the moss-covered trunk of a fallen oak, and stepped out onto the road, still singing. She carried a basket of green herbs over her arm.

The maiden realized that there was someone on the road. She stopped singing, stopped walking, and looked at Hyvarnion. In that moment, their eyes met, and he felt that he was enchanted. The maiden was as beautiful to look upon as she was to listen to. He slipped from his horse, knelt before her, and asked her name. It was Rivanone. He told her his name, and he asked if he might walk beside her, as they were going on the same road. She smiled and said yes.

As they walked in the green wood, they talked of babies and old men, of the winter that had brought sorrow and hunger, of those who had died and been buried without a priest, but with hope of the resurrection. They talked of the spring that had brought sunlight and filled the pastures with lush grass and the forests with herbs and their hearts with hope. They talked of the moon and the stars and the planets and the music of the spheres. He realized as they talked that she was as wise as she was beautiful. Then she began to sing, and he joined his voice to hers, and the two voices became one song, merging together like two drops of water or two flames. He fell in love with her as they sang, and she with him. Soon they were married, and before long they had a son.

Hearing the beginning of their story, you expect them to live happily ever after, in a house filled with music and laughter and children and grandchildren after them. But that was not their story. Their son was born blind. They named him Hervé, which means bitterness. Around the time Hervé was weaned, Hyvarnion died.

For the sake of Hervé, Rivanone did her best to push away the darkness that filled her heart and to find the strength to live without her beloved Hyvarnion. She sang of her grief to the child, filling his life with her poetry and song as well as her sorrow.

The year Hervé turned seven years of age, Rivanone had a decision to make. It was time for

Hervé to leave her and to learn a trade while living with another family. Yet when she thought of sending Hervé away, she was overcome by darkness that neither song nor prayer could drive away. She had lost Hyvarnion already. She didn't see how she could live in the world alone, without Hervé.

She considered keeping him with her a little longer. She could teach him the use of herbs. He had already learned a great deal, just from being with her as she gathered herbs and made tinctures and poultices. She could teach him enough to launch him on a career as a physician.

She knew, though, that he wanted to sing. His voice was like his father's, full of the sound of sunlight and summer rain, gentle and sweet and strong. She decided to commit Hervé to the care of a holy man named Arthian. Arthian would teach Hervé to play the harp and to sing. Hervé would be a bard like his father, and Rivanone would live out her years as an anchoress, dying to the world so that she might live with God.

Arthian taught Hervé how to sing and how to beg. Every day, no matter the weather, Hervé wandered the streets with a begging bowl and a small white dog. He would sing, and people would hear in his voice all the grief and joy of their lives, the longing for the past that was gone, and around the longing was something almost like hope. As they listened, they wiped tears from their eyes, and they dropped coins in Hervé's begging bowl.

While it was common at the time for blind people to make their living as beggars, that was not what Rivanone had in mind when she committed Hervé to Arthian. She spoke to Arthian softly, gently, pleading with him to teach Hervé to play the harp and to conduct himself like the bard of a king. Rivanone spoke to Arthian intensely, fiercely, demanding that he give her son dignity. He told her she was a fool.

Rivanone took Hervé from Arthian and sent him to her brother, the monk Gourvoyed. Gourvoyed had opened a school in the forest near the town of Plouvein. There, Hervé lived as a hermit, with a boy named Guiharan as his disciple and companion and guide.

At the school, Hervé learned the Holy Gospel and the rules of monastic life as easily as he had learned the use of herbs when he was young. Pilgrims who stopped at Plouvein for shelter on their way to the holy sites would stay to hear him sing the services of the Church.

Then came the year of the great darkness. During Bright Week, after the celebration of the Glorious Resurrection of the God-Man, night fell, a strange fog obscured the sky, and day never came.

Without the sun, there was neither warmth nor light. Seed was sown, but never sprouted. Chickens laid no eggs. There was frost on the ground at Pentecost. The land was filled with hunger and fear. People no longer went on pilgrimages, yet some still came to Plouvein to beg for food and shelter. Gourvoyed welcomed everyone who came in the name of God. Whatever food he had, he shared. No one was full, but somehow there was always enough to keep every soul alive.

Through it all, Hervé sang. He sang the services of the Church at the appointed times, and in the evenings, after they shared a meager supper, he sang the songs of sorrow he had learned from his mother.

When the darkness finally passed, many of the men who had come to Plouvein so they might eat stayed to study and work and pray. Soon the school became a monastery.

Then came plague. People who lived in the surrounding forests brought their sick so that the monks could pray for them and anoint them with holy oil and care for them until they died. To keep the sickness from spreading, Gourvoyed set up a hospice apart from the guest houses and the dormitories. Yet in the first year of the plague, many of the monks died, Hervé's friend and companion Guiharan among them. In the second year, Gourvoyed died, and Hervé became the head of the school and the abbot of the monastery.

Just as people who were sick came to the monastery, birds and forest creatures who were sick and injured came to Hervé's cell. Hervé knew when they arrived. He would take the animal onto his lap and examine it with gentle fingers. He would splint broken wings, apply wine and honey to open wounds, administer tinctures to animals whose breathing was labored. When the animals were whole, Hervé would bless them, and they would bow to him and leave.

During the plague, a lone wolf came to Plouvein. People began seeing it lurking around their homes, menacing their fowl and frightening their children. Hervé called to the wolf. When he felt the great animal brush against his leg, he led it to his cell. The wolf submitted to his examination. Hervé found a festering sore on its shoulder, large and deep. He made a bed for the wolf in his own cell, and he treated it with kindness and herbs for many weeks. As its shoulder healed, the wolf began following Hervé wherever he went. It shared his cell, and it shared his meals of bread and lentils.

Yet even after the wolf's shoulder was entirely healed, some darkness remained in its heart. As Hervé was preparing to harness the monastery's ox to plow the fields one day, he left the wolf and the ox alone together for just a moment. The wolf attacked the ox. The ox bellowed. The wolf snarled. Hervé's guide cried out in fear. Hervé commanded silence and asked what was happening. There was more shouting, more bellowing, more snarling, and then silence. By then, it was too late. The ox would die. Hervé could not save it.

The monks demanded the death of the wolf, but Hervé would not hear of it. He collected his thoughts, then sang a song of sorrow and loss. The wolf was still. He laid down at Hervé's feet, and Hervé forgave the wolf. Yet the wolf needed more than forgiveness, and the fields needed to be plowed. So Hervé preached a sermon to the wolf, a sermon about mercy and repentance and the need to plow the fields so that the monks would have food for the winter. As Hervé preached, the wolf whimpered; as he pronounced the amen, the wolf howled a song of repentance to the skies. As its song faded, the wolf walked to the yoke that still laid on the ground and began pawing at it. Hervé blessed the wolf, then yoked it to the plow. From that day, until the end of its life, the wolf plowed the fields in place of the ox.

After some time, the plague passed, and Hervé moved the monastery to Leon, where the air was more wholesome than Plouvein. As the monks loaded the mules for the journey, birds and forest animals came to watch. As the mule train departed, the birds flew over their heads, and the squirrels and rabbits and other small creatures hopped beside them until they reached the main road. Hervé stopped and blessed them. They bowed, each in their own way, and turned back to the forest.

The bishop thought the abbot of a large and well-respected monastery should be a priest, but Hervé refused to be ordained. He declined all earthly honors. Even so, when a solemn assembly was called to determine whether Conomor the Cursed, king of Dumnonia and prince of Poher, should be anathematized, Hervé participated in the assembly.

After that time, darkness and plague came to Leon. Hervé was numbered among the sick, but he recovered. When his strength returned, he set out with a small group of monks to find a new site for the monastery. They went west, and found a hilltop at Lanhouarneau, near the sea where the air blew fresh and clean. There was a river for water, and land for grazing and plowing. There, Hervé and his monks built their new monastery. The monastery was blessed with light and health and plenty, and Hervé's songs were filled with peace.

Although he was not yet old, Hervé had never fully recovered from the sickness that had afflicted him at Leon. He became weak and frail, and when he was near to death, the monks took it in turns to sit watch with him.

On a moonless summer night when the sky was bright with stars and a cooling breeze blew gently through the windows, the monks sitting with Hervé felt a change in the air, as if a curtain had been pulled back. They began to hear music. A great light filled the room, and choirs of angels filled the sky, welcoming the blind bard to join them in heavenly song. So Hervé died and was buried at Lanhouarneau with honor and tears and love.

St. Hervé

In the year 536, a volcanic eruption filled the sky with smoke and ash. Night fell, and day wouldn't return for nearly two years. All of Europe, along with the Middle East and parts of Asia, suffered from cold and famine. Before the world had recovered, in the year 540, another enormous volcanic eruption occurred. In the years that followed, Brittany suffered from epidemic diseases that killed many of those who had survived the great darkness. It may have been the bubonic plague, which swept the world from 541 through 549, or it may have been yellow fever or some other infectious disease. Whatever the cause, the population of Brittany collapsed during the life of St. Hervé.

Hervé is said to have written the beautiful Breton hymn *Kantik ar Baradoz*, the Song of Paradise. The hymn is still sung at funerals in Brittany. I think perhaps it is a song he learned from his mother.

Prayer
O Hervé, minstrel and teacher of the Faith, your sweet voice enlightened the darkness though you were born without the gift of sight. Pray that the light of Christ may ever dispel the new pagan darkness from our lands, that God may be glorified.

St. Etheldreda
Born around 630, Exning, Suffolk, East Anglia
Died 679, Ely, Cambridgeshire, East Anglia

FEAST DAY JUNE 23

Etheldreda, the lady of Ely, kept her eyes closed and her body still. She wanted to hear ... what? or whom? She knew not. She knew only that something had been distracting her from her prayers last night, and so, at last, she had turned to God and his Mother for answers. She had gone to the Gospel book and prayed for knowledge. Then she had opened the book, pointed to the page, and read the words that she found under her finger.

> *Amen, amen dico tibi: cum esses junior, cingebas te, et ambulabas ubi volebas: cum autem senueris, extendes manus tuas, et alius te cinget, et ducet quo tu non vis. Hoc autem dixit significans qua morte clarificaturus esset Deum. Et cum hoc dixisset, dicit ei: Sequere me.*
>
> *It is true, it is true what I tell you: When you were young, you tied yourself, and you walked where you chose. When you are old, you will hold out your hands and someone else will tie you and take you where you choose not. This he said to show the death*

that would glorify God. And when he had said this, he said to him, Follow me!

She read it again, to make sure she had made no mistake, then read it the third time. There was no mistake. God and his Mother were warning her.

The words rang in her mind as she left the tower that served as her oratory and crawled into her bed in the hall. They were carried in the murmuring voices of the water and the songs of the frogs who offered their hymns through the night. Now, in the first gray light of morning, they echoed in the songs of the birds. "Who is coming?" she whispered. "And when?"

"My lady?" asked Wendreda.

Etheldreda quit pretending to sleep and sat up. "Wendreda, summon Brother Owine at once," she said.

"Yes, my lady," she said. She nodded towards the serving girl closest to the door.

Moments later, Owine stepped through the door and bowed to the ground.

"Get up, Brother Owine," said Etheldeda, "and tell me, have you any word of emissaries coming to see us?"

"No, my lady."

"After Compline, God and his Mother told me that someone is coming to tie my hands and take me where I choose not to go. I must know who, and why, and where they will take me."

Owine sighed deeply. "My lady, you inquired of them using the Gospel?"

"I did, Brother Owine, just as my sisters taught me, before they went to Gaul. That is why I begged Father to make you teach me to read, so that I might know the Word of God."

"Yes, my lady."

"So, Brother Owine, you must ask our people to tell us who is coming across the fen."

"Yes, my lady." Owine took his cloak from a peg, pinned it in place, and went out the door into the early morning light.

The sky was growing dark when Owine returned, and the stars were beginning to appear in the places appointed for them. Owine looked at the sky, crossed himself, and asked the virgin Queen of Heaven for her blessing. Then he entered the hall and bowed to his own virgin queen, Etheldreda.

"Get up, Brother Owine, and speak."

"Two days hence, my lady, emissaries from your uncle the King will arrive at the edge of the fens. There they will camp for the night. The next morning, they will come here to take you to marry Ecgfrith, King of Decia and heir to Northumbria."

Etheldreda stared at him as if he were speaking a foreign tongue. The song of the frogs seemed to fade into silence.

"Tell me again," she said, and Owine repeated what he had said.

"No," Etheldreda said. "No. I am a widow with land of my own. I need no husband, nor can anyone require me to take a husband. I will not go."

"If you will not go, my lady, they will take you."

"Then I will leave before they get here, and they will not find me."

Owine raised an eyebrow. "Where will you go?" he asked.

"I will go to my cousin Botolph at Ikanhoh."

"Brother Botolph?"

"Yes, Brother Botolph. My father's sister-son."

"Are you quite certain that Brother Botolph would not send you to your uncle?"

"He wants me to be a nun. He told me that himself."

"He may want you to be a nun, but he can ill afford the enmity of the king." Owine paused, considering his words. "Speaking plainly, my lady, you are not a nun. When your husband died, you could have chosen to take the veil. It would not have been denied you then. Yet you chose to come here rather than to join your sisters at the monastery in Gaul. Again when your kinswoman Hilda founded her monastery at Whitby, you chose to stay here."

Etheldreda clenched her jaw. Her father told her, when he gave the monk Owine into her service as her chief steward, that he was as wise and cunning as a dragon. She was not required to like what he told her, and she was not required to do as he wished, but she must always allow him to speak plainly, and she must consider his advice.

She considered it, and she liked it not. "No," she said. "I will not go with them. I will go to Whitby, and I will take the veil. Once I have taken the veil, they would not dare take me."

"My lady, they would dare."

"But why, Brother Owine? Why?"

"My lady, your king and father needed an alliance with the Gyrwas, to defend his land from Mercia, and so you married Lord Tonberct. Your king and uncle needs an alliance with Northumbria, and so you will marry Prince Ecgfrith."

Etheldreda watched the smoke curling up from the fire to the ceiling. "Brother Owine," she said, "my lord Tonberct already had an heir, and so had no need of one from me. When I told him I had promised myself to God, he was content to live with me as the Holy Joseph lived with God's Mother. Does this Ecgfrith have an heir?"

"Prince Ecgfrith is not yet a man."

"How old is he, Brother Owine?"

"Fifteen years, my lady."

"By God's wounds, Brother Owine! He is not a man, but nor is he a child. He will want to take me to wife."

"When the emissaries arrive, my lady, we

will negotiate the terms of the marriage. He will accept what is agreed to, as will you."

"If I refuse?"

"My lady, you will not be allowed to refuse."

"St. Thekla preserved her maidenhead by having God seal her into a stone."

"Indeed. And you will preserve your maidenhead by sealing a marriage contract."

Etheldreda scowled. "Could I not pay the emissaries to go away?" she asked. "I have jewels and silks and gold and fine linen."

"You do, and you could," said Owine. "But there would be other emissaries, and what would you give them?"

Etheldreda sat in silence for a long time. Finally, she spoke. "Tell me, Brother Owine, what must I do?"

"Reeve Evgetus and I have already started. The men of your uncle's court believe the fens are an impoverished land, filled with demons and bandits and ill omens. We will show your uncle's emissaries a land of peace and plenty, made so by the power of your virtue and your virginity. They will learn that, with the help of God and the

Virgin Queen of Heaven, you have cast out the demons, overcome the bandits, and filled the hungry with good things."

"They will believe that?"

"They will see it with their own eyes. As your chief magistrate and reeve, Evgetus will greet the emissaries as they enter the fens. He will inform the emissaries that God told you, our God-protected virgin queen, that they were coming. He will welcome them in your name and under your protection. He will give them your command to leave their horses and their weapons there, with your grooms and armorers, and he will bring them to you."

"Will they not protest?"

"They will protest, my lady, and Reeve Evgetus will remind them that they are your guests, under your protection, and that without your blessing and your guides, they will be lost in the fens and beset by demons, and their bodies will never be found."

Etheldreda sat without moving. Smoke drifted up from the fire, and the sound of frogs filled the silence. A dog barked, and the frogs went silent. When they started singing again, Etheldreda spoke. "Why should we guide them here? Why not guide them to where they will die in the fens?"

"My lady, if those men return not to your uncle, he will send others. We may be able to persuade these men to be your servants, and not enemies who will bind your hands and take you where you choose not to go."

Etheldreda spat on the fire. "Go on," she said. "Tell me how you will persuade them."

"We will persuade them with your wealth and your power, with blessings and curses and threats and omens. By this time tomorrow, I will know the names of every man of them, and which of them still honor the old gods. Your shepherd Wurt keeps a raven as a pet. As Reeve Evgetus leads them to the river, they will hear the raven croaking. They may even see it fly over them as they get on the boat. They will disembark at Turbotsey, and from there they will come here as in a procession. Young girls will throw flowers in their path. Old women will call them by name and bless the wombs of their wives in honor of our virgin queen. Poets with flagons of wine will chant verses extolling your power and wealth and virtue. There will be pigs roasting on spits along the way, and baskets of fruit, and platters piled high with custard tarts colored with saffron.

There will be casks of ale, and if I have time there will be fountains flowing with wine."

Etheldreda considered his words. "You are certain there will be reason to celebrate?" she asked.

"I am, my lady," Owine said. "By the time the emissaries arrive here, they will be filled with awe and fear. They will know Ely as a land of wealth and power, a blessed land with you as its God-protected virgin queen."

Etheldreda sighed deeply. "So let it be," she said.

Wendreda paused for a moment. The morning songs of the birds blended with Etheldreda's voice as she chanted her morning prayers in the oratory. A woman of the fens, Wendreda had been given to Etheldreda's father, Anna, when he was made king of East Anglia, and she had served Etheldreda ever since. She knew every nuance of Etheldreda's voice, she understood her every motion, and she knew how to clothe her in splendor.

She had laid out for her lady a linen underdress, as blue as the summer sky. The overdress of red silk, embroidered around the hem with gold thread, with a pair of fine gold and garnet brooches to fasten the shoulders. An ornate leather belt. To hang from the belt, a key, a knife with a jeweled hilt, and a small leather bag closed with a ring of ivory. To hang from her neck, three necklaces of various lengths, with beads of glass and amber and gold. For her head, a red silk cap, a red and yellow fillet, and a yellow veil trimmed with blue. For her feet, intricately worked leather boots. Over it all, a cloak of fine wool, embroidered with flowers and birds, lined with fur, and fastened with a large jeweled brooch. When Etheldreda took the veil, if she ever took the veil, she would need none of this. For now, though, for today, it was good that she had it.

Owine looked over the finery. "Only three necklaces?" he asked.

"Yes, my lord. The lord bishop has counseled her to wear no more than three necklaces at a time, for modesty's sake."

"Today is not a day for modesty," he said. "She must wear no fewer than seven necklaces. Ten would be better. If one of those chests holds a jeweled pendant, have her wear that as well."

It was the sixth hour when one of the serving boys ran into the hall. "They are coming!" he said.

Owine clapped his hands. "Everyone to your places!"

Wendreda had placed a chair on a platform on the north side of the hall, set it with silk cushions and draped it in silk. She had one of the serving boys hang a large shield on the wall behind it. To the east, richly embroidered drapes hung from the ceiling and pooled on the floor, separating the hall from the oratory. A wood fire burned brightly between the platform and the door, and beeswax candles surrounded the platform, their fragrance filling the hall.

Etheldreda stepped up onto the platform and arranged herself in the chair. Wendreda adjusted her cloak, then stepped back. Her lady's face was radiant in the candlelight. Her finery caught the light of the fire. She could be the model for the Virgin Queen of Heaven in a great cathedral, enthroned in the apse above the altar. She could equally well be Sunna, the old goddess of the sun, the goddess of healing, the goddess Wendreda had worshipped before she knew of the Christian God. The shield could be a nimbus for a saint, or it could be Sunna's shield.

Etheldreda shifted in the chair. Wendreda stepped behind her. The other maidservants took their places on either side. Silence filled the hall like smoke.

The dogs in their kennels barked and growled. The kennel boy hushed them.

Etheldreda's thoughts swirled. The men were coming. They were coming to tie her and take her to a place she chose not. She would not leave Ely if she could choose to stay. Her lord Tondberct gave her this island on the morning after they wed. The island and its people belonged to her, and she to them. If Brother Owine had not told them to guide her uncle's men to her, the peat bogs would have taken the men, pulling them and their and horses into the depths, never to be seen again.

As the men approached, the words from the Gospel ran through Etheldreda's mind. The men had come to tie her and take her away from the fens, away from her land and her people. She rested her arms on the arms of the chair. She would go, but they would not take her. With the help of God and his Mother, she would go freely, not as a prisoner, but as a queen.

Brother Owine entered the hall and bowed to the ground.

"Arise," said Etheldreda. He rose, then stepped aside so the emissaries could enter. They stepped across the threshold, then stopped, staring at the woman seated on the chair beyond the hearth fire, the woman who glowed with the fire of the sun.

Etheldreda held her breath. Slowly, the men bowed to the ground. She waited until Owine moved his right hand ever so slightly. "Arise," she said.

They rose. One stepped forward from the rest. "Speak," said Etheldreda.

"My lady, I bring you greetings from your uncle, the King."

"When you return to my uncle, the heir of my father," she replied, "you will bring him my greetings."

"My lady, your uncle, the King, requires that you attend him yourself. We have come to bring you to him."

"Is that all he requires?" she asked. "That I bring him my greetings?"

"It is all that he requires of us," he replied,

"to bring you to him."

"What does he require of me?"

"That, my lady, he shall tell you when you arrive at his court."

Etheldreda stirred. Her jewels flashed. There was a rushing sound as Wurt's raven landed just outside the open door. He hopped into the hall, walked past the fire to where Etheldreda sat, then hopped up onto the platform. Etheldreda nodded to the raven, who bowed to her.

"My servants have set a table before my door," she told the emissaries. "You and my servant Owine, who serves as lord of my household, will sit at the table, and you shall tell him all that you know of the plans that my uncle, the King, has for me. You and my servant Owine will reach an agreement on the terms of all things concerning me at my uncle's court.

"Until my servant Owine has agreed, and you have sworn, I shall not move."

The emissaries bowed again to her, then rose. The eldest of them looked at the raven, then nodded towards it and walked backwards out the door. The rest of the emissaries did the same. Owine followed them. The table was waiting.

As the sun moved across the sky, the serving girls kept the emissaries' cups filled with wine and ale and mead enough to make talk flow like the river. They brought silver plates filled with cheese and white bread, with pots of butter and honey. They brought boards piled high with ginger cakes and apple tarts redolent with cinnamon, and glass bowls filled with tiny roasted songbirds. Wendreda brought wine and bread and cheese to her lady, who ate the bread and drank the wine and tossed bits of cheese to the raven.

The sky was bright with stars when Owine entered the hall. He held a parchment in his hand. Again, he bowed to the ground.

"Arise," said Etheldreda. "Have you an agreement?"

"I have," said Owine. As he handed her the parchment, Wendreda brought a small table and a candle.

According to the agreement, these emissaries were to be sworn protectors of the virginity of Etheldreda, the queen and lady of Ely. She would marry Prince Ecgfrith, but the marriage would not be consummated. They would kill any man who would dare attempt to take her by force or by seduction. Her oath to preserve her virginity for her God and her lands, and their oath to protect her, would be inviolable, unless she herself chose to have the oaths dissolved, with the blessing of a bishop.

She would keep all lands and possessions given her by her father Anna and her husband Tonberct, in her own right, including her Gospel book, which she had received from Cuthbert's monastery. Her reeve Evgetus would remain in Ely to manage the commons, to administer the courts, and to receive the customary payments from the fen people.

She would bring with her two hounds, all her clothing and jewels and bedding, her books, her bed, her taefl board and the game pieces of bone and amber, a barrel of imported wine, two grooms, three maidservants, five kitchen servants, her princeps domus the monk Owine, her personal maid Wendreda, and clothing and bedding for all the servants. She would send servants to arrange wagons and draft horses across the river, as well as fine riding horses for herself, Owine, and Wendreda. In addition, the Gospel book would be carried on a litter by two boys dressed in fine linen, with four stout men to guard it. There would be no exchange of hostages to guarantee the agreement. God Himself would enforce its terms.

Around the edges of the parchment, in the margins, were runes that she did not recognize. "Brother Owine!" she said. "What are these? What is their meaning? What power have they?"

"They have such meaning and such power as the emissaries give them," he said. "That is all."

Owine sent a child to summon the emissaries into the hall, which was filled with the sounds and smells of the coming feast. As the men bowed to the floor, Etheldreda rose and walked towards the oratory. A pair of serving boys pulled back the drapes so that she could enter. The raven followed her. The emissaries rose and followed the raven, and Owine followed the emissaries.

The oratory was filled with shadows and the smell of incense. A table was set against the east wall. The table was covered with silk embroidered with gold, and the Gospel book and candles were upon it. On the Gospel book was the parchment that contained the agreement Owine and the emissaries had negotiated.

The emissaries came forward one at a time,

bowed to the ground before Etheldreda, then bowed before the Gospel book and kissed it. Each then recited every detail in the parchment that laid upon the book. At the end of each recitation, Etheldreda said, "If you should fail in the least part of this agreement, or if you should seek to alter its terms in any way, or to allow anyone else to do so, at that moment, all that you own, and your wife and your children, will be forfeit to me, and my God will strike you dead and cast your soul into the abyss, where you will suffer forever with the devil and all his accursed companions."

Each said, "So have I sworn. So will it be." They bowed again to the Gospel, and again to Etheldreda, before leaving the oratory.

When the last emissary had sworn and bowed and left the nave, the raven bowed towards Etheldreda. It walked into the hall, out the door, and flew into the night.

Owine said, "It is done, my lady. I can do no more."

"It is enough, Brother Owine. Let us join the feast."

It was three days to prepare and pack, then four

more days to move all the people and goods to Turbotsey, and from there up the river by boat. Another 10 days to travel overland to Rendlesham, where Etheldreda's king and uncle Aethelwold kept his court.

Etheldreda and Wendreda sat on cushions on the ground, listening to the serving women singing as they went about their work and to the men shouting in the hall. Etheldreda fidgeted with her necklaces. The warmth of the amber beads calmed her. "I have not heard Brother Owine's voice," she said.

"The man with the strongest position has the least need to shout," responded Wendreda.

Eventually the shouting subsided to talk, and after some time, the talk was punctuated with laughter. As a serving woman brought Etheldreda and Wendreda cherries and wine, the men came out of the hall.

"Etheldreda, queen and lady of Ely, daughter of my brother, your father would be proud of your strength and your cunning. I have confirmed the agreement made at Ely in all its details. Tomorrow, when you marry Prince Ecgfrith, you shall have a husband who is not a husband. That which is yours will not become his, neither your lands nor your maidenhead, until you so choose, and your choice is confirmed by a bishop."

Etheldreda nodded. "So may it be."

The marriage agreement said nothing about where they would live. Etheldreda expected it would be in her uncle's royal compound in Rendlesham, which was near enough to Ely. Instead, she would be going with her husband to his father's royal compound in York.

"York, Brother Owine! York! The king and my husband decided that I would go to York! They did not ask whether it pleased me to go there. It is too far from Ely. I will not go."

"Prince Ecgfrith is heir to Northumbria, my lady," said Owine. "He needs to be in his own lands."

"Then let him go. I will stay here."

Owine considered his next words. "The Queen of Heaven told you that you would be taken to a place you did not choose."

"I thought that was the wedding, Brother Owine. Not York. York is too far from my lands.

It is too far from the sea, too far from the fens. The air in York is bad. It stinks of butchers and tanners. In York, Brother Owine, the frogs don't sing."

Owine was silent.

"Brother Owine, have I no choice?"

"None, my lady."

"By God's wounds, then, I will go to York. But I will not abide there forever."

At York, Etheldreda and Ecgfrith developed a deep friendship with the monk Wilfrid, who served Ecgfrith as Owine served Etheldreda. On winter afternoons, Etheldreda and Ecgfrith would sit near the fire in the hall. Ecgfrith would read aloud from books chosen by Wilfrid while Etheldreda embroidered stoles and cuffs in silk thread and gold on fine linen. She sent them to priests throughout their land, and she gave a set to Wilfrid when he was ordained priest.

Ecgfrith, for his part, asked Wilfrid and Owine and Wendreda to teach him how to delight his wife. He learned to praise her wisdom and piety rather than her beauty, and he gave her necklaces and fine jewels that caught the sun and brought light into her eyes.

Wilfrid spoke for the Roman side at the Council of Whitby, then went to Gaul to be made bishop. It was five years before he returned. With him came the news that Etheldreda feared. The king of Northumbria had died. Ecgfrith was now the king of Northumbria. He would want an heir.

He was not so blunt, of course. He spoke to her with tenderness. He showered her with gifts. As the days passed and the seasons changed, he wooed her with all the good things a king could give a woman. She responded with deep and maternal affection, and reminded him that her maidenhead belonged to God, and was not hers to give away.

Ecgfrith grew impatient. He would not take her by force. He could, of course. The people would understand it, and the Church would allow it. But there were eleven men remaining of her sworn protectors, eleven men who feared God and Heaven's Queen. They had taken an oath. They would kill him if he tried to take his wife, whether he was king or not. That he knew.

At last he summoned Bishop Wilfrid.

The two men sat congenially, drinking spiced wine and talking of many things before King Ecgfrith got to the point. "My lord Bishop," he said, "you know that my beloved Etheldreda has taken an oath of virginity. You must release her from that oath, so that she can fulfill her marital debt and provide for me an heir."

Wilfrid nodded. "I have often wondered when we would have this conversation, you and I."

"So you will free her from this oath?"

"My lord, I cannot," said the bishop.

"The wedding contract says that you can free her."

"It says that, at her request and with her consent, I can free her and her protectors from their oaths. Without her consent, I can do nothing. And she will not consent."

"Bishop Wilfrid, she respects you as her lord and father. If you talk to her, she will change her mind."

"She will not change her mind."

The king stared into his cup. "A chest of gold and two of silver, together with 5 hides of land, would make a worthy gift, my lord bishop, to celebrate the consummation of the marriage."

"I will take no gift," Wilfrid said, "but I will talk to her. Although, your grace, the conversation may not go to your liking."

Etheldreda was blunt. "My husband is a king, my lord bishop. If he needs a woman, he can take a mistress, or a whore. If he needs an heir, he can choose one of his sister-sons. If he must have an heir of his own flesh, our marriage can be annulled, and he can take another wife."

"He can," said Wilfrid. "Yet he wants no other wife. He wants you, my lady, and it is only a matter of time before he decides that he will have you."

"His men will kill him if he tries."

"My lady Etheldreda, it has been ten years since they took the oath at Ely. Seven of them have died since. One is missing a leg, another is blind. Those that remain will not be able to protect you if he imprisons them or kills them."

"He cannot do that."

The bishop did not respond. Etheldreda waited in silence, fidgeting with her necklaces, staring into an unwanted future. At last she could wait no longer. "My lord bishop," she said, "what shall I do?"

"Your husband's aunt Ebbe is the abbess of the monastery at Coldingham," Wilfrid said. "Go to Coldingham now. I will follow you, and you can take the veil from my hands. Your husband would not be so rash as to lay siege to his aunt's monastery."

Etheldreda nodded. "Leave me now," she said. "I will see you again at Coldingham." As he left, she clapped for a servant. "Summon Brother Owine and Wendreda," she said.

Owine and Wendreda entered and bowed. "Rise," said Etheldreda. "I will be leaving tomorrow," she said. "I am going to the monastery at Coldingham, where I will take the veil. My husband must not know I am going."

"I will begin packing now," said Wendreda.

"You will not go with me," said Etheldreda. "While I ride north to Coldingham, you and Brother Owine will ride south, to the fens. Your heart is there, Wendreda. You must go and take up the life of an anchoress in the place where you were born, where the salt water and the fresh water meet."

"My lady," Wendreda interrupted.

Etheldreda waved her hand.

"Not now, Wendreda. Brother Owine, go with her, and ensure that she arrives safely. Take all my necklaces, all my jewels, and use them to provide for her whatever she needs. Whatever is left, you must give to the poor of the fens."

"Yes, my lady," said Owine.

"Then you, Brother Owine," Etheldreda said, "once Wendreda is settled, what is your wish? Would you come back and serve my uncle?"

"My lady, when you have taken the veil, I wish to return to the monastery that I left to serve your father and you."

"So be it," said Etheldreda. "Before we leave, there is the matter of manumission. Wendreda must be free. We can record the manumission in my Gospel book."

"My lady," said Owine, "manumission requires a bishop and witnesses."

Etheldreda frowned. "How many witnesses?"

"Two should be enough."

"Summon Bishop Wilfrid and two of my

sworn protectors to meet us at the church, and we will free Wendreda tonight. Once that is done, they must stage horses and supplies for you and Wendreda behind the springhouse beyond the hill. You will leave at first light tomorrow. Have two others take supplies and wait for me at the inn on the road to Coldingham. I will ride out as if on an errand of mercy and meet them there. We will ride hard for Coldingham, to get there before my husband knows we are gone."

"Your protectors know how to ride hard and sleep rough," said Wendreda. "Can you learn that art so quickly?"

"I can, because I must," said Etheldreda. "As for you two, I expect that my lord husband will follow you to the fens."

"Yes, my lady," said Owine. "I will, with your leave, take your Gospel book with me when we go, to protect Wendreda's freedom and to ensure that our lord and king follows us."

"Let it be so," said Etheldreda.

Etheldreda had not fully appreciated how fast three people could travel without carts or cooks. It took but three days to travel from York to

Coldingham. Etheldreda looked more like a beggar than a queen when they arrived at the monastery, which stood on a high cliff above the ocean. Her protectors remained on their horses as she dismounted and knocked at the monastery gate.

"I am Etheldreda, daughter of King Anna, niece of King Aethelwold, and wife of King Ecgfrith," she told the porter who opened the window in the gate. "I would see the abbess." The porter nodded and closed the window. Etheldreda stood and waited, listening for the porter, listening to the sound of the ocean below, smelling the salt in the air. When the porter returned to admit her, Etheldreda turned to her protectors. "I am under God's protection now," she said. "You may return to my uncle, your king."

Etheldreda sat with Abbess Ebbe near the fire and told her all that had happened since she was taken from Ely and married to Ecgfrith. As she finished her story, Ebbe asked one question: "Why took you not the veil when your first husband died?"

Etheldreda shook her head. "I know not, my lady abbess." The long silence between them was filled with the quiet sounds of the monastery and of the ocean beyond. "I have wanted to take the veil since I was a child. Yet it seems that I have loved my silks and necklaces more than I loved God." She paused. "I have given them up. I know now that if I keep them, then I cannot keep my maidenhead."

"Oh, my daughter, preserving your maidenhead is only the first and least of the ascetic labors that will be required of you. I will shelter you here, and you will share in our common life and labors. You will wear wool and not linen, and you will sit in the lowest place at our meals. We will decide after a time whether you will take the veil."

Etheldreda started to object, and then she stopped herself. If she were to be a nun, she had to give up more than her necklaces. She had to give up being a queen.

As Etheldreda had expected, when Ecgfrith realized that she and Owine and Wendreda were all gone, he and his men headed south towards the fens to retrieve them. They found no trace of Etheldreda nor her servants. At last, though, they were themselves found by a spy from York. His message was brief: Etheldreda was in Coldingham.

Five days later, Wilfrid arrived in Coldingham. He had with him a young boy from the fens who had a message for the abbess. Armed men were coming to take Etheldreda, the wife of the king. He thought they were perhaps two days behind them.

The next morning, Etheldreda received the veil from Wilfrid's hands. "Now you must flee," the abbess told Etheldreda. "I will not be able to keep you safe from my nephew."

"I will go to Ely. Having looked for me there once without finding me, he will not look again."

The abbess nodded. "Sisters Sewara and Sewenna were born in the fens. They have begged leave to go with you, if you will have them," she said. "I would advise you to have them. Though one may be overpowered, two can defend themselves, and a cord of three strands is not quickly broken."

"I will have them," Etheldreda said.

The tide was coming in as the three women left the monastery, and the waves were beginning to crash against the cliffs below. The women turned south and walked down the hill to where the roads diverged. "Before we choose a road," said Sewara, "let us go to the top of Coldeburch's Head. From there, we can see many miles in every direction, and we will know which road your lord husband takes, and which way we should go."

Etheldreda acknowledged Sewara's wisdom. The three women left the road and walked together to the place where the rocks of Coldeburch's Head jutted out of the surrounding rocks and sand. There they found a faint path and began climbing. By the time they were halfway to the top, the water was lapping at the base of the hill. They stopped briefly, considering whether they might be stranded by the incoming tide, then went on.

As they reached the top, Sewenna gasped and pointed to the south. A group of horsemen were on the road in the distance, riding hard towards Coldingham.

"It is the king," breathed Etheldreda. The men could not have heard her. It was not possible, yet they reined in their horses and looked towards Coldeburch's Head, where the women stood against the sky. The men seemed to take counsel with each other, then as one they turned off the road. The horses picked their way carefully around tide pools and broken rocks as they made their way towards Coldeburch's Head, towards the women.

The women stood on the crest of the hill and prayed. As they prayed, the waters rose. The hill became an island, and water churned around it.

When Ecgfrith and his men came near the hill, they dismounted and hobbled their horses, then waited for the tide to go out.

It did not go out. For seven days, the men watched and waited. For seven days, the women stood and prayed. Finally, the king understood that God and his Mother had spoken. He would not have Etheldreda as his wife.

The women watched the men break camp and ride away. They sat on the ground, exhausted from fear and sleeplessness, weak from hunger and thirst. Slowly, the waves began to still, and the water began to ebb away.

"I have not the strength to climb down the hill," Sewara said.

"Nor I," said Sewenna.

"You must pray for water," said Abbess Ebbe.

Etheldreda turned towards the abbess's voice, but no one was there. The other two seemed not to have heard the abbess.

"Sister Etheldreda," said the abbess more urgently, "pray."

Etheldreda knelt on the rock and began to pour out her heart to God and his Mother. As she prayed, a spring of water broke forth close to her, pouring out sparkling sweet water, as much as they could drink.

After many days and more miracles, Etheldreda and her companions arrived at the border of the fens. "We will not take the main road," she said. "Someone may be looking for us. We will take the path to the summer pastures." Sewenna and Sewara assented, and the three turned aside from the road and entered the green darkness of the trees by a narrow path. Etheldreda breathed deeply. The air carried the smells of trees and earth and water and home.

As they walked, Etheldreda began to

consider how they would cross the river to the island. They could, perhaps, find a coracle along the bank and take it across. Yet this time of year, the water was likely to run fast and deep.

Ahead, the trees opened up into the pasture. A man sat on a moss-covered stone beside the path. Sewara noticed him first. "Sister Etheldreda, my lady, look."

Etheldreda looked. "Evgetus, my reeve!" she called out.

The man stood, then bowed low. "My lady Etheldreda, your servant, Brother Owine, sent word to expect you this day."

Etheldreda laughed. "How would Brother Owine know?" she asked. "Where is he now?"

"He is at the monastery of St. Chad, my lady. Yet he has eyes and ears in many places."

"Reeve Evgetus, did Brother Owine tell you to have a boat ready to take us to Ely?"

The reeve's eyes twinkled. "He said to have two boats ready. There is one fitted out for a queen, and another for a nun."

"As you can see by my garments, Reeve Evgetus, I am a nun. Take me and my companions to the boat for a nun."

"Yes, my lady," said the reeve.

It was a quick journey from the pasture to the river, and across the river to Turbotsey. From there, Reeve Evgetus walked with the women to Etheldreda's hall. "I will leave you here," he said, and turned back towards the river.

Two servant girls stepped out the door and bowed. "Welcome home, my lady," they said to Etheldreda.

Etheldreda and her companions entered the hall. The floor was covered with fragrant herbs and new rushes. A pot of stew bubbled over the peat fire. Smoke curled up towards the ceiling.

Etheldreda stepped into the oratory to give thanks. On the table against the east wall was a Gospel book. Her Gospel book. She stared at the book. Then, slowly, she lowered herself to the floor and cried.

The next morning, after the three nuns chanted the morning prayers in the oratory, Sewara looked at Sewenna, who nodded.

"My lady," Sewara said, "Sister Sewenna

and I are nuns and not anchoresses. When the bishop arrives, it is our desire that he bless this building to be our monastery, and you to be our abbess."

"What? No!" said Etheldreda. "You were there when I took the veil. You heard me renounce all my wealth and all worldly authority. I cannot be the abbess."

"Sister Etheldreda," said Sewenna.

"No, stop," said Etheldreda. "Let us not argue. Let us ask God and his Mother whether I should be abbess."

"Let it be so," said Sewara.

Etheldreda prayed for guidance and illumination, then opened the Gospel book and pointed to a verse.

"Read it," said Sewenna.

Etheldreda read: *dixit autem Maria ecce ancilla Domini fiat mihi secundum verbum tuum et discessit ab illa angelus.* "Then said Mary, behold the maidservant of the Lord. Be it to me according to your word. And the angel left her."

When Bishop Wilfred came to the fens, Sister Etheldreda became the Abbess of Ely.

Now, six years later, Abbess Etheldreda ruled over a large and prosperous double monastery. She sat at the table in the refectory and listened to a young nun reading the Scriptures as everyone ate. She was reading that very passage, the one that had made her the Abbess of Ely. So much had changed since then. The building that had served as her hall was now a church. The timbers of the oratory had been replaced with stone. Her sister Sexburga had joined the monastery after her son came of age. And Brother Owine! The year after she had returned, he joined her monastery as well.

Of all the blessings she had received since taking the veil, the only one that pained her was the tumor that had developed under her jaw.

When the meal was over and Etheldreda had given thanks, Sewenna approached her and bowed. "My lady abbess, my lord Brother Cynefrid would like to talk with you."

"Of course he would," Etheldreda said. "I will see him in the courtyard."

Cynefrid, a monk of Ely and a skilled physician, told his abbess that he needed to remove the tumor from her jaw. She insisted that the tumor was a gift from God. It reminded her of all the necklaces she had worn, of her vanity and pride. If she did no penance in this life, then she would find herself with the rich man in the next life, across the chasm from Lazarus.

"You eat but one meal a day. You take cold baths and wear wool and not linen. Is that not penance enough?" asked Cynefrid.

"If it were enough, would God have sent this tumor?" she snapped. "Besides, God's Mother has told me that a pestilence is coming, and when it is here, it will be time for me to die. Not before."

The next day, Sister Sexburga joined her voice to the doctor's. "Perhaps this tumor is an ordinary tumor and not from God at all," she said. "I also wore fine necklaces when we were young, and I have no tumor."

"Perhaps your love for your necklaces was less than mine," said Etheldreda, "or your repentance has been greater."

"If I had that tumor instead of you, you would command me to let Brother Cynefrid treat it," Sexburga replied. "In humility, then, you must be obedient to the command that you would give me."

Etheldreda glared at her sister. "If the surgery kills me, Sexburga, my sister, you must bury me in a plain wooden coffin with the other nuns. You may wrap me in a linen shroud, if you must, but you will not bury me as if I were a queen. There will be no cups, no jewels, not a single bead. This is my command."

"Yes, Abbess," said Sexburga to her sister. "It will be so."

Etheldreda survived the surgery, but the tumor grew back. She refused a second surgery, and as she was less able to drink or eat, she grew thinner and weaker. When the pestilence came to the fens that year, Abbess Etheldreda died. She was buried according to her wishes, and her sister Sexburga succeeded her as Abbess of Ely.

St. Etheldreda

Etheldreda was likely the youngest daughter of Anna, King of East Anglia. Because of her prominence, and the importance of her family, her life is documented in many records dating from near her time, including Bede's *Ecclesiastical History*. In modern history books, her name is most often given as Æthelthryth. In the Catholic tradition, she is best known as St. Audrey.

Some sources say that Etheldreda had a sister named Wendreda, although she is not mentioned by Bede nor any other contemporary sources. Wendreda seems to have been a nun and healer from March, perhaps the abbess of a small community on the border between the saltwater and fresh water in the fens. A medieval church in March is dedicated to St. Wendreda, which is the only church in the world with that dedication, and the only certain evidence that Wendreda ever existed. If she did exist, the lack of contemporary documentation meant she could not have been Etheldreda's sister, but was perhaps a member of her household.

Bede identified Owine as Etheldreda's princeps domus. The title denoted the master of a queen's household. Owine had been a monk in St. Chad's monastery before serving Etheldreda.

When she founded the double monastery in Ely, he became a monk there.

Besides the mention in Bede, Owine is known from the base of a cross that was destroyed during the iconoclasm of Henry VIII. The base survived in a field, where it was used to tether livestock. Inscribed in the base are the words, "Lucem tuam Ovino da Deus et requiem Amen," which means "O God, give your light and rest to Owine. Amen."

The agreement Owine negotiated between Etheldreda and her uncle's men, to protect her virginity, is my own invention. The old stories say that King Ecgfrith pleaded with Bishop Wilfrid to make Etheldreda give up her oath of virginity and be a proper wife to him. That made no sense to me, given the power of husbands and kings of the time, and I wanted King Ecgfrith to have a reason for his reluctance to take his wife.

Etheldreda having her own Gospel book is also my invention. Her embroidering vestments is from the historical record; she embroidered a stole and cuffs for St. Cuthbert. The miraculous tide around Coldeburch's Head is also in the oldest sources.

Prayer
O Virgin Queen, you have suffered the pains of ascetic struggle and thus gained grace through the necklace of your virtues, to heal diseases of both body and soul, to drive out demons, and to protect all those that suffer: O venerable Mother Etheldreda, pray for us that we may obtain healing and great mercy.

St. Cenydd of Wales
Born 6th century, Loughor, Glamorgan, Wales
Died 6th century, Gower Peninsula, Wales

FEAST DAY AUGUST 1

The woman sat on a stool in front of her doorway. Although the air was cold, the sun gave enough warmth that she could sit and spin. The tide was coming in, and her husband would soon be home. She was content.

As she spun, she looked out over the tide flats to Worm's Head. A vast number of gulls were flocking around the long, rocky outcropping, as if every gull in the world had come for some great festival. They would wheel up into the air and dive back down, fly away, then return.

She stood up and stretched her back a bit. Then, after putting her spinning back inside the cottage, she walked down towards the water to watch the gulls.

Over supper, she told her husband what she had seen. He, too, had seen the gulls wheeling in the sky. "Tomorrow," he said, "when the tide is out, I'll go over to Worm's Head and see what caught their eyes."

When the sun came up the next morning,

the frost was heavy on the ground. The woman and her husband said their prayers, then tended the animals, as they did every morning. After they broke their fast, they went out to watch the tide go out as the gulls circled and swooped over Worm's Head.

"It's still cold," said the woman. "You'll want your cloak and mittens."

The man got his cloak and mittens from the cottage, then set out walking toward Worm's Head.

The woman knew he would be wet to his knees, and cold, when he got back. She added a bit more wood to the fire, so the cottage would be warm. She considered what else she might do before her husband returned and decided that she was too distracted by the mystery of the gulls to do anything but spin. So she spun, and sang a song of waiting, and watched until her husband came walking back across the tide flats. He was carrying a large basket in his arms. The gulls were following him, wheeling away and returning.

She walked towards her husband as far as the ground was dry, and stood, watching, as he approached. When he was close enough that she could hear him, he called out to her. "My wife, come here. It seems that we have a son."

"We have what?" she called back, lifting her skirts and walking out towards him, her footprints glistening with dampness. "What is in the basket?"

"A baby. A boy. A son."

She stopped in her tracks. They had been married 20 years, and she had never been with child. Her womb was closed. She was barren. When her husband got to where she stood, she looked into his eyes. "My lord husband, do not mock me," she said.

"I do not mock you, my love," he said. "Look in the basket."

She pulled back the fine linen cloth that covered the basket. Inside, an infant was tucked under a soft fur, lying in a cloud of down and feathers. The babe looked up at her. His face was beautiful, his eyes as blue as the sky.

The gulls continued to wheel around them as they took the boy to the cottage. "My breasts are dry," said the woman. "Nor can I think of any woman here with a babe at the breast, who could suckle him. How will we feed him?"

"The priest will have milk from his goats,"

her husband said.

"Oh, my blessing, the babe can't suck from a goat's teat!"

"No, never, my love! Until he can drink from a cup, we can dip a cloth in milk, and let him suck milk from the cloth."

She nodded.

"While you get the lad settled, my love, I'll walk up to the priest's cottage, and see whether he'll help us feed the lad."

The man walked in with a jug of milk. "My wife! My love! Our priest is an angel! He will give our lad all the milk he needs. And listen! The priest will baptize him on Sunday!"

His wife didn't turn to him. She was singing softly, a song of a mother's love, a song of hope and sorrow. When the song was done, she sat in silence for a moment. Her husband's eyes were bright with tears. Finally, she spoke. "My blessing, look here," she said. She had swaddled the babe in the linen that had covered his basket. As her husband put the milk on the table and took off his cloak, she unwrapped the babe, picked him up, and handed him, naked, to her husband.

The babe's right leg was bent and folded, with the calf against the back of his thigh. It was as tight as if it had been trussed.

The man sat on the bench by the fire and held the infant on his lap. "When I was on Worm's Head," he said, "I examined the babe's entire body. Except for the leg, the child is perfect."

His wife looked at the child, then at her husband. "Why?" she asked softly.

"Why is his leg bent?"

"No, my blessing. The leg is surely a gift of God's mercy. I want to know why he came to us in a basket."

The man pulled the babe close. "I am not a seer, and yet I think that the babe's father saw the leg and ordered him drowned."

His wife nodded. "The one who wants him dead must not hear of him," she said.

When the babe was baptized, he was given the name Cenydd. He drank milk from the priest's goats, first sucking it from a cloth, then sipping from a cup. Such a cup it was! The innkeeper just up the river had a brass cup made, shaped like a breast, with a spout shaped like a nipple low on one side, as a gift to the lad.

With the cup, the innkeeper brought a story that had come down the river. At Christmas, he said, Arthur, the King, had called his tributaries to celebrate the feast with him. One of the men, Dihoc by name, feared neither God nor man. He brought with him his daughter, who was great with his own child. On the Feast of the Holy Innocents, the child was born. His right leg was bent backwards, as if the calf was fused to the thigh. Dihoc ordered the child to be thrown into the River Loughor and drowned.

The midwives, though, fashioned a basket out of willow, wrapped the babe in linen and fur, and set the basket in the river with tears and with prayers that the basket would carry the babe to safety and not to death. As they watched the basket float away, they sang a blessing, a song of hope and a mother's love.

As Cenydd grew, his parents taught him to pray and to sing, and they took him to church as often as they could. They always called the priest their angel. Just as he had provided milk to nourish

Cenydd's body when he was a babe, the priest began to nourish Cenydd's soul and mind with holy writings. He taught the boy to read the Psalms and the Gospels and to sing all the services of the church.

When Cenydd was 18, he told his foster parents and the priest that he wanted to live as a hermit. The priest gave him his blessing and told him of a place where there was a bit of dry land surrounded by willows and reeds. Cenydd took leave of his foster parents and made his way towards the place the priest had directed him to.

When he found the land the priest had described, he built a hut. Before long, a man appeared, asking to live with him as his servant. Giving thanks to God, Cenydd received him. Having a servant meant that he could devote more time to prayer, and he could more readily extend hospitality to those who came to receive his wisdom and his prayer.

After some time, a group of nine robbers heard stories of Cenydd. They knew he would have little in the way of wealth, but it amused them to visit Cenydd to see what they might receive from him. When they came to his hut, he welcomed them as cherished guests and invited them into his hut to eat with him. The robbers accepted the invitation, and, out of respect for Cenydd's holiness, they left their weapons outside, leaning against the wall.

Cenydd's servant did not share his master's holiness. As he sat outside the hut, he looked at the swords and spears and lances. They were fine weapons, chased with intricate designs, and his heart began to covet them.

After the robbers had eaten their fill of fish and leeks and drunk their fill of mead, they asked Cenydd to share his wisdom with him. He talked with them about the richness of poverty and the glory of humility. When he finished, three of the robbers took out recorders and began to play a merry tune. "Stop!" the oldest of the robbers said sharply. "Do not offend our host by playing songs from a brothel. Do you not know other songs?"

"I remember the songs my mother taught me," said the robber with gray eyes, "songs about springtime and winter, planting and harvest."

"Play those," the oldest robber said. So the gray-eyed robber played. Soon, the other two joined in, and the rest of the robbers began to sing. Cenydd, realizing with delight that he knew the song as well, added his voice to theirs.

As Cenydd's servant listened to Cenydd and the robbers singing, he knew they would not hear him moving about outside. He took one of the lances and hid it in a secret place.

Many hours later, the robbers bowed and took their leave. As they picked up their weapons, the gray-eyed one realized that his lance was missing. He asked Cenydd's servant where it was, and the servant swore he hadn't seen it. The robber began to threaten him, and the servant shouted to Cenydd and begged him to bring the cup from which he'd drunk the angel's milk. He would swear on that cup, by all that is holy, that he had not touched the lance.

The moment he swore the false oath, he shuddered and fell to the ground. Then, shaking and whimpering, he got up and looked at the robbers. It seemed to the robbers that he did not know that they were men. He backed away, then turned and ran off into the darkness.

Seven years later, Cenydd received a deacon with a message. The deacon told him that his servant had been seen in the woodlands near Bishop Dewi. He was living like a wild beast, unclothed except for his long hair that covered him. In pity, Cenydd prayed for him, and at that moment, his servant was restored to his right mind. He made his way back to Cenydd, who received him as the shepherd received the lost sheep, and as the father received his prodigal son.

Days passed, and weeks, and seasons. Then all the abbots and bishops of Wales were summoned to a council at Llanddewi Brefi. On their way to the council, Bishop Dewi, together with Bishops Teilo and Padam, stopped at Cenydd's hut. He received them as he received all his guests, with joy and hospitality. After they had prayed and eaten, they joined their voices in songs of beauty and holiness and awe. Then the bishops told him why they had come. Although Cenydd was neither abbot nor bishop, he was known to be a holy man. They wanted him to attend the council.

As he listened to their invitation, he shook his head. "You see my leg, my lord bishops. How should I get there before the council ends?" At that, Bishop Dewi prayed for him, and Cenydd's leg straightened, so that he could walk like other men.

Cenydd looked at his leg, then at Bishop Dewi. "Why did you do that?" he asked. "God blessed me with this bent leg from my birth, and you would take it away from me?" He turned away from the bishops, and cried out, "My Lord and my God, return your blessing to your servant, and make my leg as it was before, that I may be preserved from sin all the days of my life." With that, his leg bent itself back as it had been. "Now, my good bishops," he said, "may God grant you safe travels to Llanddewi Brefi. It appears that I will remain here."

So he did, for the rest of his days.

St. Cenydd of Wales

In England, St. Cenydd's name would be written as St. Kenneth. All we know about him for sure is that he lived in Wales in the sixth century, and he was widely known and widely regarded as a holy man.

Any more details come from two sources recorded long after his death. One was either found or made up by Iolo Morganwg, a 19th century Welsh poet who wrote stories of Welsh saints and heroes and passed them off as ancient documents. Morganwg's story says that St. Cenydd was the son of St. Gildas the Wise, that he lived as a hermit, that he founded monasteries, that he married and had sons of his own.

The other story is far more interesting. It was first recorded in the early 14th century by John of Tynemouth, who traveled across England and Wales, collecting stories of saints. In this story, St. Cenydd is the son and grandson of Dihoc, a tributary of King Arthur. Dihoc orders the child drowned, and the midwives, fearing God more than they feared Dihoc, place the child in a basket and set him in the river. When the basket washes up on Worm's Head, the seagulls stop the peasant and his wife from taking the child. The child stays on the island. Angels bring him milk from heaven in a brass bell shaped like a woman's breast. When he is 18, an angel tells him to leave the island and become a hermit. The hut he made of willow and reeds, the servant, the robbers, the healing by Bishop Dewi (known now as Dewi Sant Cymru, or, in English, St. David of Wales) and the unhealing, all come from that story.

The story, of course, is not historical. Yet such a story could have grown out of events that really happened. I tried to reconstruct what those events might have been.

Prayer
Renouncing the world you sought out a desert on an island off the Gower where you could pray. O righteous Cenydd, as we rejoice in your God-pleasing asceticism, beseech Christ our God that He will save our souls.

St. Pimen the Much-Ailing

Born in the second half of the 11th century, near Kyiv, Ukraine
Died 1110, Kyiv, Ukraine

FEAST DAY AUGUST 7

Pimen's parents slipped quietly into his room, as they had done so many times over the years since he was born. His mother sat on the bench by his bed. Humming a lullaby, she gently pushed his long, dark hair away from his face, then made the sign of the cross over his forehead. His father picked up a stray birch leaf from the floor, left over from the branches that had filled the house on Pentecost.

Pimen stirred and moaned. His eyelids fluttered.

"Pimen," said his father. "Pimen, are you awake?"

"Yes, Father," Pimen said.

"Pimen, the weather is fair. If you still desire it, we will make a pilgrimage to the Monastery of the Caves and pray there for your healing."

"Father, yes Father! Yes, I desire to make that pilgrimage with all my heart." He rested a moment before speaking again, softly. "Perhaps, if God wills, I can stay there as a monk."

"If God wills," his mother said.

While Pimen's father oversaw the loading of a small cart for the journey, his mother gathered a basket of roses. When all was ready, she and her husband helped Pimen in. She set the basket of roses at his feet, tucked pillows around him, and put a fur over his lap before settling herself into the cart beside him. The servant adjusted the mule's harness, then took the rein in his hands, clucked to the mule, and started walking. Pimen's father walked alongside the cart.

Near the port on the Desna River, a birch grove grew between the road and the river. The branches were adorned with ribbons and flower garlands that other travelers had offered to the river spirits, or to the Archangel Michael. "Stop here," said Pimen's mother. She got out of the cart and picked up the basket of roses. "You go on," she said to her husband. "I'll offer prayers for a safe journey and meet you at the ferry."

Her husband watched her walk to the trees, then nodded to his servant. They continued to the port, where the ferry to Kyiv was already waiting.

The journey was difficult for Pimen. When they got to the monastery, Pimen's father lifted him from the cart, carried him into the chamber in the guest house that had been assigned to them, and laid him in a bed to recover.

The chamber was simple and spare, adequate for their needs: beds, benches, and a small table, all made of oak. In the corner was a shelf with an icon of St. Michael. The icon was draped with an embroidered cloth, and an oil lamp burned in front of it. The room smelled faintly of incense. The distant voices of monks chanting hymns to the Theotokos drifted into the room.

Pimen had fallen into a fitful sleep when there was a knock at the door. Pimen's father opened the watch-window to see who was there.

"I am Father Agapetus," said the monk. "I am the monastery physician. The guest master told me that a pilgrim in this room is ailing."

"That would be our son," said Pimen's father, opening the door and stepping aside. Father Agapetus entered, bringing with him the smell of incense. "His name is Pimen," his father continued. "He has been ailing since his birth, before he ever set a foot on the ground, before he had hair that might have been taken and used against him. The healers have been unable to drive his infirmities from him. We brought him here, that he might be healed by the prayers of the holy monks and the saints."

Father Agapetus walked to Pimen's bed. He watched the young man's chest rise and fall with his breath. He was thin, but not skeletal. His face was pale, yet there was color in his lips. He laid his hand on Pimen's forehead. There was no fever, no rash, nothing that would make him a danger to the monastery.

"When you bring him to the church, wait in the nave when the service is over. I'll bring priests to pray for him, and oil for anointing."

Pimen's mother blinked back tears. "Thank you," she said, her voice barely more than a whisper.

The church was already crowded with pilgrims when Pimen and his family entered. A choir of monks stood in the back, chanting psalms. Clouds of incense filled the air. Angels and saints covered the walls, and gold leaf gleamed in the light of a thousand candles. The Theotokos stood at prayer on the back wall of the apse, with her Son in a field of stars over her bosom. Christ Pantocrator looked over all from the center of the vaulted ceiling.

Pimen and his father found a place along the south wall of the nave, where Pimen could sit on the stone bench when he could no longer stand. His mother stood on the north side of the nave, with the women. When she caught a glimpse of her son through the crowd, his face was radiant.

After the service, as the pilgrims left the church, Father Agapetus and six priest monks approached Pimen and his father. A deacon carried the Gospel book.

"Pimen," said Father Agapetus, "We will pray for you, that God may deliver you from your infirmities."

"What? No!" said Pimen.

With that word, everything stopped. No one moved. No one spoke. Father Agapetus wondered if perhaps an exorcism might be needed before the prayers of anointing.

Pimen realized the monks and his parents were all staring at him. "I do not wish to be healed," he said. "God gave me these afflictions for my salvation. Because of the infirmity of my body, I have been spared infirmities that would afflict my soul. Do not pray for my healing, my lords. Pray for my salvation and make me a brother of this monastery."

"If you have received your illness as a divine gift," said the oldest of the priests, "we will not ask God to take it from you. God's gifts are irrevocable. Yet we cannot simply tonsure you a monk. Hegumen Nikon will have to speak with you, to determine if you have the strength to take on this holy calling."

"I have the strength," said Pimen.

"It may be that you do," responded the priest. "I will arrange an audience with Hegumen Nikon tomorrow. Tonight, you and your parents will return to your quarters and rest."

"My lord," said Pimen. "May I stay here in the nave tonight, and pray?"

The priest looked at him thoughtfully. "You may," he said.

Soon, the nave was silent and empty. Pimen stood and prayed. For a time, he thought he dreamed. It was a dream he'd often had in his illness. Angels descended around him. They were dressed as monks; their hands and faces were bright in the darkness. They were singing words that Pimen didn't know. One of the angels held a Gospel book. Another angel set a pair of scissors on the Gospel book. The angel pointed at the scissors, then at Pimen. Pimen picked up the scissors and handed them to the angel. The angel set the scissors back on the Gospel book, then pointed again. Again, Pimen picked up the scissors and handed them to the angel. A third time, the angel set the scissors on the Gospel book. A third time, Pimen picked up the scissors and handed them to the angel.

The angel took the scissors and cut off Pimen's hair. Another angel gathered up the hair and placed it in the reliquary of the Venerable St. Theodosius. Then, singing, the angels dressed Pimen in the garments of a monk. They gave him a prayer rope and a candle, and each of the angels gave him a kiss of peace. The last angel spoke to Pimen in his own language. "By God's mercy, you will be afflicted in the flesh until the day of your death."

The monks came to see who might be singing in the night. As they entered the nave, the voices faded away. Only Pimen was there, clothed in monastic garments, with a candle in his hand.

One of the monks went to get Hegumen Nikon. Another went to get Father Agapetus. Pimen stood without moving, watching the candle flame dance as the angels had danced around him.

Hegumen Nikon shook his head. "Father Agapetus," he said, "it appears that I am not to be given a choice to accept this brother or not." Then he turned to Pimen. "You are now a brother of this monastery, and you will henceforth be called Father Pimen. You have died to your old life. You will live here, in sobriety, chastity, poverty, piety, and obedience, until the end of your days."

"Yes, my lord. I will."

One morning a few weeks after the angels had tonsured Father Pimen, Father Agapetus sat on the bench in Father Pimen's cell. "There is another monk, my brother, who is also severely afflicted in the body. You may have met him, the monk Vratislav."

"I know him," said Father Pimen.

"Like you, he has been assigned a private cell, out of mercy for his sufferings," said Father Agapetus. "Yet you are not hermits. If the two of you shared a cell, you could comfort each other, and those assigned to attend your needs, and his, could serve you more easily."

Father Pimen nodded.

"Would it be agreeable to you, then," asked Father Agapetus, "if Father Vratislav were to share your cell?"

"Yes, my lord," said Father Pimen. "I would welcome Father Vratislav."

Father Vratislav was much loved by the brethren, and for many months, both he and Father Pimen were well cared for. Yet there is little pleasure in carrying trays and emptying chamber pots and all the other tasks required to attend those who are weak and afflicted. Over time, their attendants, young men of noble families, came to find this service intolerable. They would leave the monks Pimen and Vratislav without food or water for two or three days at a time.

"I thirst," said Father Vratislav.

"May God be glorified," said Father Pimen. "Our Lord and Savior said those words from the Cross. Truly, we are blessed to share in his sufferings."

"I do not feel blessed," said Father Vratislav. "I feel that I might die."

"What joy that would be!" said Father Pimen. Father Vratislav coughed. "Oh, my beloved Father Vratislav! The holy apostle Paul said that, when we share in our Savior's suffering and become like him in his death, we will most certainly receive the resurrection from the dead, and joy and glory in the Kingdom that has no end!"

"What of our brothers who neglect us?" said Father Vratislav. "At the last judgment, will they not be numbered among the goats, because they did not give drink to the thirsty or visit the sick?"

Father Pimen frowned. "My brother, you speak true. But what can we do?"

"God sent angels to you, Father Pimen, and they pray for you always before God's throne. Ask God to heal me. He will hear your prayer and heal me, and when I am whole, I will serve you with joy and gratitude until the day of your death."

Father Pimen considered his brother's words. They seemed wise, so he prayed to the angels, and then to the Theotokos and to St. Anthony, whose icons were in the corner of the cell. He asked them to pray for his brother, the monk Vratislav, who was afflicted in body, and to heal him and deliver him from every infirmity.

By God's grace and mercy, Father Vratislav was healed. As he had promised, he served Father Pimen with joy and gratitude. After a time, though, the joy became a distant memory. He found much pleasure in reading spiritual books and talking with other monks about spiritual matters, and little in keeping Father Pimen clean and comfortable. As he began to neglect Father Pimen, his former affliction returned to him. There were days that he needed someone to help him tend to his own needs, and the monks who had delighted in conversation with him found no joy in serving him.

When Father Vratislav came to his senses, he said, "Behold, how good it was, how pleasant, when Father Pimen and I dwelled together in unity! We used to hold sweet converse together; we walked in fellowship. Yet now, in my affliction, I am alone and hungry! I will go back to my brother Pimen and say to him: My brother, I have sinned against heaven and against you. Heal me, and I will be your servant." So he got up and went to Father Pimen's cell. Prostrating himself beside Father Pimen's bed, he began to weep.

"My beloved brother," said Father Pimen, "why so many tears?"

"Oh, Father Pimen, my friend and my brother!" he said, "I have broken my promise to you and to God." He took a deep, shuddering breath. "I left you in pain, hungry, and alone, and God has chastised me by visiting my former illness on me. If I had your strength, my brother, I would accept this illness for my salvation! But I am weak, Father Pimen. I cannot bear the pain."

"Then let me pray for you, my brother, that God will heal you again."

"Oh, Father Pimen! I desire that with all my heart! If you heal me, I will be your servant, and never falter, until the end of my days." A long silence fell between them. Finally, Father Vratislav spoke again. "Even so, my brother," he said, "I am afraid."

"What do you fear?"

"If you heal me, Father Pimen," he said, his voice a hoarse whisper, "how will I be saved? I will have nothing to offer God at the last judgment."

"Do you not understand, Father Vratislav? When you serve the sick, you and they will be judged together. You and they will receive the same reward."

"I don't understand."

"My brother, hear me! At the last judgment, those you served will walk with you to the judgment seat, and they will tell our Lord Christ how you served them, and He will say to you, 'Come, you who are blessed by my Father! Enter into the Kingdom that was prepared for you before all ages!'"

With those words, he signed Father Vratislav with the cross, and Father Vratislav was healed.

So it was that the monks Pimen and Vratislav shared the same cell for 20 years, laboring together for their salvation. On the Sunday after Pentecost, when the church was still filled with the branches of birch trees, Father Pimen woke up entirely healed in his body. With great joy, he went to church and told the other monks that he would die later that day, as the angel had foretold. Having made his confession the evening before, he received the Holy Mysteries, then exchanged forgiveness with all.

The monks Pimen and Vratislav walked back to their cell in silence. There was nothing that needed to be said. Father Pimen picked up his bed and carried it to the place where he wished to be buried. There he laid himself on his bed. Father Vratislav sat on the ground beside him. The silence between them was filled with waiting, and the waiting became music, and the music was filled with voices pure and sweet. Father Pimen recognized the voices. "The angels have come for me," he said, then he spoke no more.

Father Vratislav closed Father Pimen's eyes and wept.

St. Pimen the Much-Ailing

St. Anthony founded the monastery of the Kiev Caves only 40 years before Pimen arrived there with his parents, when Christianity was still new in Ukraine. While the Ukrainian people had given up the old gods, they had retained rituals that provided protection from the lesser spirits that were thought to inhabit water and trees and fields. It seems likely that the angels in the story of St. Pimen gathered up his hair and put it in a reliquary to ensure that it could not be used by malevolent powers to do him harm.

The sources for St. Pimen's life tell of the brother he healed, but they do not give him a name. I chose the name Vratislav for him. The name comes from the Slavic elements *vratiti,* which means "to return" and *slava,* which means "glory".

Prayer
By a flood of tears you made the desert fertile, and your longing for God brought forth fruits in abundance. By the radiance of miracles you illumined the whole universe! O our holy father Pimen, pray to Christ our God to save our souls.

St. Theodore of Tobolsk
Born 1895, Tobolsk, Tyumen Oblast, Russia
Died 1937, Tobolsk, Tyumen Oblast, Union of Soviet Socialist Republics

FEAST DAY AUGUST 30

Whether it was from sleeping on the cold floor at the cathedral, or from the bad air at home near the river, who could tell? Whatever the reason, Theodore was often sick. Usually it was no more than a cold, and who thinks anything of it when a child has a cold?

One winter morning when Theodore was 13 years old, though, it was more than a cold. The other children were up and dressed. Eugenia was already bringing tea and porridge to the table when little Natalya pulled at Elizaveta's skirt. "Theodore is sick again, Mama," she said. "He won't wake up."

Elizaveta sighed. She put down the sweater she was mending, pushed back the curtain from the women's corner, and knelt down next to the bench where Theodore was sleeping. He moved restlessly, tangled in his blanket. He felt warmer than the petch, the great masonry stove that was the heart of the house.

"Theodore, wake up!" she said. He didn't

answer.

"I'll fetch the doctor," said Theodore's father, Ivan, who was already putting on his boots.

The doctor said it was rheumatism. The best treatment was to keep him warm until the fever and pain passed.

Ivan lifted him into the sleeping space on the petch, and Elizaveta tucked blankets around him. Soon, the fever passed. Yet the pain remained, and with the pain was paralysis. Theodore could not move his legs.

"He must stay on the petch," Elizaveta insisted. "The warmth soothes the pain."

"It soothes the pain until I have to lift him down and carry him to the table or the privy," said Ivan. "It is even worse for him when I lift him up again. I cannot move him without hurting him."

"The fever left him but three days ago. It will take time for the petch to draw out the pain and paralysis. He should stay on the petch a few days longer."

Ivan sighed. "We will keep him on the

petch, then, until the doctor returns. If he tells us to keep Theodore on the petch until the pain is gone, then we will keep him there. Otherwise, we will put a bed next to the petch. He will be warm there."

After examining Theodore, the doctor sat with Ivan and Elizaveta at the table in the Beautiful Corner. "There is nothing more I can do for him," the doctor said. "The condition seems to be permanent. Keep him warm, but you must not lift him up onto the petch, Ivan. It will not help, and you could be injured. It is not worth the risk. Make him as comfortable as you can, and have faith in God."

Theodore was settled into the iron-framed bed next to the petch. Sometimes, when he tried to adjust his own position in the bed, the pain would stab like a knife, and he would scream, and his sisters would cry. Sometimes he buried his face in his pillow and cried from the pain, hoping that no one would notice. Eugenia would always notice. She would take her knitting and sit next to him, singing softly until his pain and his tears subsided.

Doctors came and went. The dean of the Cathedral, Father Gleb, brought him the Holy Mysteries and blessed him and prayed for him.

Matushka Anya, Father Gleb's wife, visited him with kind words and semolina cake. Nothing changed. Theodore was still in pain. He still couldn't move his legs. He still couldn't stand. Days passed, and weeks, and years. His brothers Yuri and Grigory found jobs and wives. Eugenia likewise married. For Theodore, his bed, and his pain, were his world.

In February of 1916, before Theodore's 21st birthday, Ivan came home from work with exciting news. Their beloved Metropolitan John Maximovitch would finally be glorified as a saint. His spiritual writings, his care for the poor, his asceticism, his patience in sickness, and his miracles had all cried out for his glorification. When his relics were found to be incorrupt, the Tsar himself had told the Synod that it was his wish that the Metropolitan be glorified. At last, the Synod had agreed.

The date was set for June 10. The incorrupt relics of the soon-to-be-glorified saint would be placed in a silver reliquary, and the reliquary would be placed in a beautifully carved wooden sarcophagus. The relics would be taken to the cathedral in the kremlin, the ancient fort on the hill above the city. After the service of glorification, they would be taken in a procession to all the churches in the lower part of the city, then returned to the cathedral square where they might be venerated by all the faithful.

Or, more precisely, all the faithful who could climb the 198 steps from the lower city to the kremlin.

As the day of the service came closer, pilgrims began to fill Tobolsk. There were barons and counts, bishops and priests, monks and heiromonks, with their attendants and servants and aides. It was clear there would be no room for a common person from Tobolsk at the service.

Eugenia and Nikolai, her husband, were at the house with their baby. The baby was named Ivan for Eugenia's father. Elizaveta sat on a bench next to the petch and held out her arms. "Come to your babushka, Vanya!" she called softly. "Come to me."

Theodore turned back to his father. "Can we at least go to the cathedral square and venerate the relics?" he pleaded.

"How can we get you there?" asked Ivan. "The pain would be terrible."

"I would willingly suffer the pain," Theodore said, "if only I could go."

Ivan watched as Vanya started walking across the room. He fell down twice before reaching his grandmother. She lifted him into her lap, and he clapped his hands.

Ivan shook his head. "You can't stand, Theodore," he said. "You can't walk."

"I know, Papa," said Theodore. He turned his head so his father wouldn't see the tears.

"Couldn't we make a stretcher?" asked Eugenia. "We could carry him, like the friends of the paralytic carried their friend to see Jesus."

"I could carry one end of the stretcher," said Nikolai.

"Papa, we could do it," said Eugenia.

"But how would we carry him up the kremlin stairs?" asked her father. "Everyone in Tobolsk will be going to the cathedral. If Theodore didn't slide off the stretcher and down the stairs, we'll get shoved off the side by the crowds."

"No one will be on the stairs early," said Nikolai. "All the rich people will be staying in the upper city anyway. Most people I know are saying they'll join the procession from down here. If we take Theodore up the stairs before the services start, we can watch the procession leave the kremlin and wait until it returns, and then we can venerate St. John's relics."

Vanya clapped his hands and laughed.

"You see?" said Eugenia. "Even Vanya agrees."

Eugenia, Nikolai, and Vanya arrived very early in the morning on the day of St. John's glorification. Yuri and Grigory and their wives arrived soon after. Elizaveta packed baskets with sour black bread and pickled cucumbers and filled a bucket with piroshki stuffed with potatoes and fish and seasoned with dill. Eugenia had brought a basket full of smoked fish, pickled carrots and radishes, and gingerbread to add to the picnic. Yuri's and Grigory's wives had filled their baskets with boiled eggs, smoked fish, cabbage dumplings, and hand pies filled with cherries. All the baskets were covered with snowy white towels bordered with elaborate red embroidery.

"The baskets are wearing their Pascha clothes, just like we are!" said Natalya, clapping her hands with joy.

Theodore smiled. "It does look like Pascha, doesn't it? That seems fitting and right, for today, we will venerate our beloved Metropolitan John, who has passed from death to life, and from earth to heaven."

Eugenia, Nikolai, and Grigory moved Theodore to the stretcher, and Elizaveta tucked a blanket over him. Nikolai and Ivan picked up the stretcher, and Grigory opened the front door.

"It's time for our Pascha procession!" said Eugenia, picking Vanya up from the floor.

As they stepped out of the house, Theodore gasped, whether from pain or joy, he didn't know. All he knew was that he felt as though he, like Metropolitan John, had passed from earth to heaven.

At the foot of the kremlin stairs, they stopped. There were a few men in black robes halfway up the stairs, and an old woman surrounded by young children a little way behind them. "As long as the procession doesn't start coming down the stairs now," said Ivan, "we should be fine."

"Why don't the two of you set the stretcher down," said Yuri. "Grigory and I will take it up the stairs." Two years older than Theodore, Yuri had always been the tallest and the strongest of the boys in the family. Nikolai and Ivan gently set the stretcher down for the handoff. As Grigory and Yuri picked it up, Nikolai positioned himself on the left side of the stretcher with Natalya, and Ivan and Elizaveta stood on the right side. Together, they would ensure that Theodore didn't fall.

As they started up, Eugenia walked behind the stretcher, carrying Vanya and singing, "Holy God, Holy Mighty, Holy Immortal One!" The others joined in as they made their way to the top of the stairs.

Once they were inside the kremlin, Eugenia and Elizaveta chose a spot on the grass, not far from the church, to spread their blankets. Grigory and Yuri set Theodore down in the middle of the blankets. Natalya pulled back the cover of the basket of gingerbread.

"Natalya!" said Elizaveta.

"Mama?"

"The Divine Liturgy is not completed."

"It hasn't started yet," Natalya said, "and we

won't be going in the church for it anyway."

"We will wait until the Liturgy is over and the procession has left the church and gone down the hill to the lower city. Then your father will bless our food, and we will eat."

Natalya folded her arms over her chest and turned to Theodore for support. He smiled at her. "Mama is right," he said. "We can wait."

As they waited, the kremlin filled with people. The wealthy and powerful went into the cathedral. The ordinary people waited outside. Grigory and Yuri positioned themselves to protect the blankets and baskets, and Theodore, from the crush of the crowd. There was a bit of a stir. Natalya stood up to see what was happening when the bells rang a peal for the arrival of the bishop. Vanya climbed into Eugenia's lap and hid his face from the sound of the bells.

Finally, the bells rang for the end of the Liturgy, and the doors of the cathedral opened. The choir came out first, not the usual cathedral choir, but a choir of monks singing the Trisagion Hymn, their voices rolling across the kremlin like distant thunder. They stood to the side to allow the monks carrying candles and the cross to leave the church and start the slow procession to all the churches in the lower part of the city. Behind the cross came icons and deep red banners that sparkled with gold embroidery. The choir stepped into the procession behind the icons. The priests and bishops followed the choir, then deacons with censers, and finally the sarcophagus holding the relics of St. John of Tobolsk, which was carried by six subdeacons. After the sarcophagus came monks with the wonder-working Abalatskaya icon of the Mother of God. As they left the church the people standing in the kremlin fell in behind them and made their way down the stairs to the lower city of Tobolsk.

As the sound of the choir faded into the distance, Natalya turned to her father. "Is it time?" she asked. Her father nodded. Everyone stood, except Theodore, as Ivan blessed the food. Then they sat on the blankets and ate.

Theodore nibbled at one of the dumplings from the plate that Eugenia had filled for him. He was in too much pain to be hungry, but he didn't want to disappoint his sister. He looked towards the cathedral. "Where do you think they'll set the relics when they get back?" he asked.

Grigory reached for a cherry hand pie. "I think they'll set everything up inside the old fortress. What do you think, Papa?"

"I don't know," he said. "The gates are small, and the crowds are large, and will be larger when the procession returns. I think they may well set up here, right in front of the cathedral doors."

As they spoke, two women and an abbot came out of the cathedral. "Look, isn't that Matushka Anya?" said Eugenia. She waved at the women, who smiled and waved back. One of them, Matushka Anya, started walking towards them.

"What a joy to see you here!" she said. "Theodore, I know you love Metropolitan John of blessed memory – or, I should call him St. John now, shouldn't I? Still, I didn't imagine that you'd be able to come. I thought you'd just watch the procession as it went by your house."

Theodore nodded. "My family carried me. They're going to bring me to the sarcophagus so I can venerate St. John properly."

"Would you like to join our lunch?" asked Elizaveta.

"I would love to," Matushka Anya replied, "but I don't have time right now."

"Eugenia made gingerbread," said Natalya.

Matushka Anya smiled at Natalya. "Oh, all right," she said. "Maybe a small piece of gingerbread." She took a piece from Eugenia's basket, then turned to Ivan. "Now, look, Ivan, do you see the abbot? I'll send him over when we get everything set up, and I'll have him bring all of you into the old fortress, where we'll set up the relics for veneration. We'll put you in a good place before the crowds arrive. It is a miracle that you are here, and the day of a saint's glorification is a day for miracles."

She took a second piece of gingerbread and hurried off. Theodore watched her go.

Soon, their lunch was over, Ivan had given thanks, and the abbot had led them to the east side of the cathedral. Matushka Anya had contrived a tall stand to rest Theodore's stretcher on, so he would be able to see the proceedings. Three monks were assigned to stay with them, to make sure that the stretcher didn't fall, and, of course, to make sure that none of the dignitaries tried to shoo them away.

Theodore fell into a dream-like state, from

fatigue and hope and pain. He thought the monks were singing within the church, but the procession wasn't back yet. Or was it? Maybe his brothers were singing, or angels, the angels around the windows in the cathedral.

Eugenia put her hand on his shoulder. "Theodore," she said. "Theodore, are you all right?" Theodore nodded. "Theodore, it's almost time. After all the clergy and the nobles have venerated the relics, the monks will carry you to the sarcophagus. Mama and Papa and the rest of us will come behind." Theodore nodded again.

When Theodore leaned towards the silver reliquary inside the open sarcophagus, pain washed over him and nearly carried him away. He fought his way back. He couldn't reach the reliquary to kiss it. He kissed his hand, then touched his hand to the reliquary. He nodded to the monks, who carried him back to where his family had been standing and set his stretcher on the stand.

He felt...he wasn't sure what he felt. Warmth was flowing through his body, like the warmth of the sleeping platform on the petch. The warmth flowed from his hand that had touched the reliquary, through his body, and into his legs. It filled his legs, then flowed out of his body, washing away fear, washing away pain.

By the time the rest of his family joined him, tears were running down Theodore's face. "Do you need to rest before we go home?" Elizaveta asked.

Theodore shook his head, struggling to find words to describe what had just happened. "My legs," he said.

"It has been too much today, hasn't it?" Eugenia said gently.

Theodore shook his head again. He wiped the tears from his face. "My legs," he said. "My pain. Gone."

"You're in pain?" said Eugenia.

"No! No pain." He took a deep breath. "The pain is gone."

Eugenia crossed herself and knelt to the ground. Theodore's parents did the same. The monks, and Grigory, and Yuri, and all the rest of the family knelt as well.

Hours later, they were all home. Father Gleb and Bishop Varnava had them wait until everyone had venerated the relics, then they came to talk to Theodore and his parents. They asked Theodore to move his legs; he couldn't so much as move his great toe. Yet there was no pain. He told Father Gleb how Matushka Anya had said it would be a day for miracles, but the only miracle he had asked for was to be able to venerate St. John's relics. Bishop Varnava said he would send a letter to the synod and to the Tsar, telling them of this, the first miracle following the glorification of St. John of Tobolsk.

It soon became Bishop Varnava's custom, when he served the All Night Vigil at the cathedral, to anoint the first few people in attendance, then have Father Gleb take over the anointings. Bishop Varnava would then go to Theodore's home, to anoint him and whoever was with him.

Now that Theodore was free of pain, he often had people with him. Those who had formerly visited him out of duty became his friends. His friends turned to him for comfort and wisdom, which he shared freely. Friends of his friends, and even complete strangers, wrote him letters, asking for spiritual advice and for his prayers. He even got letters from the Tsar and Tsarina, whose devotion to St. John matched his own. They asked Theodore to pray to St. John that their son, Alexis, might also be relieved of pain.

During Lent 1917, the Tsar abdicated. Everyone thought he would be exiled to England, but in August, he and his family were sent to Tobolsk. Tsars had been using Tobolsk as a place of exile since 1591, when Tsar Boris Gudonov exiled the Uglich bell. In more recent times, it was a way station, a processing plant. When exiles and undesirables arrived, they would be housed at the Tobolsk prison until the authorities decided what to do with them.

The Tsar and his family weren't held in the prison, though. Instead, they were moved into the grandest house in lower Tobolsk. Their servants and retainers were lodged in a lesser house across the street.

Some in Tobolsk wished for the monarchy to be restored, and some most certainly did not. Yet everyone in Tobolsk knew it was the Tsar who had insisted that their beloved St. John be glorified. They felt a debt to him for that, if for nothing else. So, although the Tsar's family were allowed no visitors, the women of Tobolsk would leave baskets of food or other small gifts for them at the servants' lodging. Often, one of the servants would slip a letter from the Tsar into Elizaveta's hand, so that she could deliver it to Theodore. Often, Elizaveta would tuck letters from Theodore to the Tsar and Tsarina into her baskets of pickled vegetables and dried fruit.

The next year, after Pascha, the Tsar and his family were moved from Tobolsk to Ekaterinburg. When word came of their deaths, Bishop Varnava offered a memorial service at the cathedral. From his bed in the lower city, Theodore heard the tolling of the bell and wept.

Before many years had passed, all of Theodore's siblings were married. It was just him and his parents in their house with its cheerful red roof. Yet the house was as full of people and song as it had always been. His siblings and their spouses and children were in and out nearly every day. The little ones would climb into the sleeping space on the petch so they could listen to the grownup talk or serve imaginary tea to imaginary guests. Neighbors would come to share real tea and stories. When it was time for a meal, Elizaveta would set as many places at the table in the Beautiful Corner as there were people in the house, and then one more, just in case. Somehow, there was always enough for all the people God sent.

In the 1930s, the government began exiling priests and monks and bishops to Tobolsk. As they arrived, they would make their way to the red-roofed house near the river to meet the one that St. John had healed from pain on the day of his glorification. They came to see evidence of a miracle, and they found the warmth of love and hospitality. They became part of the circle of people whose lives revolved around Theodore.

In July 1937, Theodore received a warning: He must quit receiving visits from the exiled clergy, or he would be arrested.

"Mama, Papa, I have never been afraid, not since the day St. John took away my pain. Yet today I am afraid that, if they come for me, they will take you as well."

"I don't believe they will," said Ivan.

"If they do" said Elizaveta, "then we will glorify God that we are counted worthy to go with you. You have been with us for 42 years, and I can't imagine life here without you."

"Don't say such things, Mama," said Theodore. "I want to imagine you here, making pickles in the summer, and serving tea to your guests, for as long as can be."

"As God wills," said his father.

Ivan and Elizaveta decided that someone should always be in the house with Theodore. They did not want him to be alone when the authorities came to arrest him.

"Grigory," Theodore said on a Saturday afternoon in late July, "you must help me. It has just occurred to me that we must burn all my letters."

Grigory nodded and opened the firebox on the petch. It was burning low. He added another stick of wood, and when that had caught, he turned to Theodore. "Start passing me the letters."

Theodore began. Some of them he kissed before handing them to Grigory. Some he opened and read once more. One after another, all the questions and pleas and prayer requests he had received over the years went into the fire. As the last letter blazed up, the cathedral bells announced the start of the vigil. Grigory stirred the ashes to make sure there was nothing left, then closed the door to the firebox.

In August, on a day when Ivan was at work and Elizaveta was off delivering a basket of black bread and fish and cabbage to a friend whose child was ill, Eugenia was sitting with Theodore, telling him about the young woman Vanya was courting. She thought there might be a wedding before the Nativity fast.

Suddenly, there was a noise on the porch and a group of men, members of the NKVD, burst into the house. Eugenia screamed. The men shouted orders, all at the same time, so it was impossible to tell what they wanted. They were all pointing their guns at Theodore.

Finally, one voice rose over the others. "Stay where you are! Do not move!"

"As I cannot move," Theodore said, "I will obey your command."

The other men began searching the house, emptying drawers, throwing books on the floor. One opened the trap door to the cellar and climbed down the ladder. There was the sound of jars being smashed.

"Stop!" shouted Eugenia. "Stop it right now. What kind of monsters are you? There is nothing in the cellar but pickled cabbage and preserved cherries and brined fish that my mother has put by for the winter." Tears were streaming down her face.

"Eugenia," Theodore said softly, "don't worry. Be at peace. Our parents won't go hungry."

"They are monsters," she said. "Monsters."

"They are our guests," Theodore said.

The men gathered up books and papers to take with them. As they left, the one who seemed to be in charge turned to Theodore. "We will return," he said.

A few days later, the men returned. This time, they knocked at the door. Eugenia answered.

"We have come for Theodore Ivanov," one of the men said formally.

"Please come in," she replied. As they entered, she turned to her brother. "Look, Theodore, your guests have returned."

"I am always happy to have guests," he said. "Would you care for tea? The samovar is on the table in the Beautiful Corner."

"I – no, no we are not staying. You must go with us."

One of the men brought in a stretcher and set it on the floor next to Theodore's bed. "Get on the stretcher," he said.

"I'm afraid I can't," said Theodore. "I have been paralyzed for many years. You'll need to move me to the stretcher if that's the way you intend to carry me out."

"Well, how do we do that?"

"I'll fold my arms across my chest, as if I'm going to receive the Eucharist, and I'll hold my head forward. One of you must stand at my shoulders, the other at my hips. A third should stand near my feet. You'll slide your arms beneath me and lift. As you can see, I'm not particularly large. If you lift at the same time, you should be able to move me easily."

Eugenia stared at the men with narrowed eyes. There was some shuffling, as they silently worked out who would stand where. Finally, three of them stood in the positions that Theodore indicated.

"Now, slide your arms under me," Theodore said. "That's right. Now, I'll count to 3, and you can all lift. One. Two. Three."

They lifted him and moved him to the stretcher, then started to pick it up.

"A moment please," said Theodore. The men stopped. "Eugenia, would you give me your red beret? When you first bobbed your hair and took to wearing berets instead of scarves, it made me sad. I've grown to like it, though. It suits you." He smiled wistfully. "Even though I don't much care for the color, the beret will remind me of you."

With tears, she kissed him, then placed the beret on his head. "May God be with you, my brother, by the prayers of St. John and of all the saints."

Theodore was taken to the prison in the kremlin. On September 11, he was sentenced to death, shot, and buried on the prison grounds.

St. Theodore of Tobolsk

Metropolitan John Maximovitch, who was glorified as St. John of Tobolsk, was born in 1651 in Czernihow Voivodeship, which was then in the Polish–Lithuanian Commonwealth and is now in Ukraine. He was made Metropolitan of Tobolsk and All Siberia in 1711, and he died in Tobolsk in 1715. He was the last Orthodox saint to be glorified before the Russian Revolution. The better-known St. John Maximovitch of Shanghai and San Francisco was related to him.

In the Soviet Union, the years 1936, 1937, and 1938 were known as the Great Terror. This was a time of mass arrests and mass executions, as Stalin tried to solidify his power and remove his enemies. In July 1937, he sent a pair of secret orders directing the arrest and execution of various anti-Soviet elements. This included Orthodox priests and bishops; 85% of Orthodox clergy in Russia were martyred during the Great Terror. It also included the friends of those considered to be anti-Soviet. That appears to have been Theodore's crime.

On October 7, 2002, the Russian Orthodox Church glorified St. Theodore of Tobolsk. In 2007, a church was consecrated in his honor in a workers' village along the Urengoy-Surgut-Chelyabinsk gas pipeline in the Khanty-

Mansiysk Diocese.

Prayer

God granted you wisdom through your ascetic struggle and remission of pain through the prayers of St. John. O holy martyr Theodore, glory of Tobolsk, pray for us, that God may grant us his great mercy.

St. Hermann of Reichenau
Born 1013, Altshausen, Swabia
Died 1054, Reichenau Abbey, Swabia

FEAST DAY SEPTEMBER 21

Preface: While much has been made of my work in astronomy and music, I think I can say, without fear of contradiction, that my most important work has been the *Chronicle of the World*, from the time of Christ to the present day.

As the author of the Chronicle, I inserted some key dates from my own life among the dates of the various kings and bishops. Yet, as my death draws near, it has occurred to me to create a small chronicle of my own life. One of my scribes is taking down my words in wax. On my death, I desire that my disciple Berthold read this chronicle and choose whether to transfer the words to parchment or to set the wax tablets in the sun and let the story of my life pass with me out of the memory of men.

The year of our Lord 1013: I was born on the 18th day of July, the fourth son of Count Wolverad II von Altshausen and his wife Hiltrud. While my mother was laboring to deliver me, there came a huge storm, and lightning struck a tree outside my mother's chamber. There was a terrifying sound, a light as bright as the sun, and the tree was split from top to bottom.

When the midwife showed me to my mother, she asked the midwife why I looked so strange. The midwife said that, when the lightning split the tree, it also split my face and mouth. She had seen such a thing before. Because of the damage, I would not be able to suckle, and so I would die. She suggested that my mother claim her right to have me exposed.

Another servant in the chamber begged leave to speak. She said that her sister had cared for a child with the same injury. It was true that the child could not suckle. Yet the child had lived. My mother sent for the sister, who confirmed everything. The servant's sister, Frau Gisela, became my nurse. She fed me and tended me as long as I lived with my parents.

The year of our Lord 1016: It became apparent, as I grew older, that the lightning had somehow damaged my limbs as well as my face and mouth. I never crawled as other children did. Frau Gisela, though, was determined that I would walk. She plied me with poultices, with practice, and with prayers to the Mother of God. With her help, and by God's grace, I took my first steps a month before my third birthday. By the time fall came, I could clothe myself and do many other ordinary things. I did them slowly, with great difficulty, and with great satisfaction.

The year of our Lord 1018: Although I could walk, I had to keep one hand on a wall, or hold someone's hand. If I didn't have that support, I fell. Oh, I fell so many, many times. As a result, I wasn't able to play with the other children in our household, and I wasn't able to do any of the tasks expected of my brothers. My father decided that, if I couldn't exercise my body, I should exercise my mind. He engaged a tutor to teach me to read. He could not have done anything that would have given me more joy! My tutor, Brother Theimo, was like an angel to me. At first, we were both frustrated because he could not understand my speech. For a time, one of my older sisters sat with us for my lessons. He would ask me a question, and I would answer, and she would tell Brother Theimo what I had said. As Brother Theimo grew familiar with my voice, he began to understand me without the need for an intermediary.

Then what joy we had! Books and words and ideas were to me the most beautiful things in all of God's creation, and I could have all of them that I wanted. Once I mastered reading, he began to teach me grammar, logic, and rhetoric.

I can imagine no childhood more idyllic than mine. I wanted for nothing. I had my nurse and my tutor, my brothers and sisters, my beloved parents, books and letters, sunshine on spring days and starry skies on cold winter nights.

The year of our Lord 1020: Brother Theimo told my father that it was time for me to go to a proper school to continue my education.

He and my father discussed the options that might be available to me. My father was a patron of the monastery at Reichenau, which was an important center for scholarship as well as sanctity. The cloister school admitted boys my age, but they didn't admit women. Frau Gisela would not be able to accompany me, and my father wasn't sure that I would be able to live here without her.

My father made several trips to the monastery, to talk first with Abbot Bern, and then with the infirmarer and the master of students. Father wanted to be sure that they all clearly understood what I would need, should I come here as a student.

Abbot Bern was pleased to accept a donation of land from my father, and pleased to accept me as a student. They agreed that two of my father's men servants, Friderich and Bertolf, would accompany me to the monastery to attend my needs. They would carry me up and down stairs, prepare my plate at meals, and assist me in other ways. Because they had known me for so long, they could understand my speech, and they would speak for me, as my sister had done, until others learned to understand me as well.

In the fall, I bade my home in Altshausen goodbye. My father and my two eldest brothers, Manegold and Lambert, traveled with me to Reichenau, along with my two men servants. Manegold had told me that the monastery was on an island, but I don't think I quite believed him until we were on the ferry going over the water to Reichenau. I felt as though I were travelling to a different world.

Of course, in some ways a monastery is a different world. We pray more and speak less, work more and eat less than people outside. In spite of this, or perhaps because of it, our hearts are filled with music, and our lives are filled with joy.

The year of our Lord 1021: When my family came for Pentecost, they brought a cart filled with offerings for the monastery: honey and beeswax, beans, and cheese. They did not bring my mother. She had only recently given birth to another son, Werner, and it was too soon for her to travel. They expected that she and Werner would come at Michaelmas.

The year of our Lord 1022: Despite my young age, I began studying the quadrivium: arithmetic, geometry, music, and astronomy. Of course, like all scholars, I continued to study grammar, logic, and rhetoric. I began seeing all the ways that the fields of learning are woven together: logic and geometry and astronomy, in particular.

A group of brothers had come to Reichenau from England, and they had taken a dislike to me. They said that God had not knit me together properly in my mother's womb. I agreed with that. My grandmother Bertha had always said that God had dropped a few stitches when he was knitting me together. From her, that was sweet and kind. From these boys, though, it sounded ugly and mean. They mimicked my speech and pretended to fall the way I often fell.

One of the novices took notice of their cruelty. He took them aside one day to tell them what had happened to me. He made up a story, saying that, when I was but five years old, I had been attacked by a bear. The bear had taken my head into its mouth, and I had grabbed its jaws and pushed them open and pulled myself free. Then I had wrestled the bear and killed it, with no weapons, only my strength and the help of God. Of course I was badly injured, but I had survived, with the damage to my face as a trophy of the encounter. He told them they must never speak of the incident to me, that if anyone asked what had happened to me, I would, in modesty and humility, tell them a fable of a lightning strike. The truth was that I had the strength of Samson, and they should be careful not to provoke me, lest I treat them as I had treated that bear.

I'm not sure if the novice ever confessed this lie to a priest. But the meanness of the English boys changed to admiration, and eventually to friendship. When we liked each other well enough that they asked me about the bear, I laughed at the story and told them about the lightning and the tree. They never believed me, though. They always believed that my injury had been caused by a bear.

The year of our Lord 1027: As I grew in stature, many things that I had once been able to do with difficulty, I could no longer do at all. I could not turn the pages in a book without either knocking the book off the stand or damaging the pages or simply waving my hand around in the air accomplishing nothing at all. Neither would my arms cooperate in clothing my body. Walking and standing likewise became impossible. Were it not for Bertolf and Friderich, I would not have been able to stay at the monastery. As my infirmity increased, they increased their care of me. Because they tended me as Frau Gisela had done when I was young, I was able to continue my studies at Reichenau. I think Abbot Bern was as relieved and as happy as I was by that state of affairs.

The year of our Lord 1028: I had grown large enough that it was no longer a simple matter to carry me from place to place. When a visitor came to the monastery in a litter, my servant Bertolf had the most brilliant idea! He and Friderich worked with one of the carpenters to create a chair with handles on it. Bertolf and Friderich could stand, one on each side of me, and carry my chair, with me in it, wherever I desired to go. If we needed to go on a narrow path, they could put walking sticks through the handles on either side. Then they could carry me, one before me and one after me. It was such a simple idea, and it allowed me to go anywhere on the island.

The year of our Lord 1029: On the 21st day of January, a day when the air was cold and the ground was hard, the relics of St. Meinrad were removed from the earth at Reichenau and translated to Einsiedeln, where St. Meinrad had been martyred for his great hospitality. I felt a certain kinship with St. Meinrad, for he had attended the cloister school here. Abbot Bern, of course, accompanied the relics on the procession to Einsiedeln, where he met scholars who helped him obtain the Latin translations of many documents that had originally been written in Arabic. I was particularly fascinated by the treatises on astronomy.

Addendum: As I began to speak of the Arabic treatises, I dozed off, and my scribe was not able to rouse me. He summoned my servants Friderich and Bertolf, who carried me to the infirmary, where I was not allowed work of any kind for many weeks. This afternoon I have at last been given a blessing to resume work on this chronicle, but I am required to limit the time and effort I put into it. With these limits, I do not know whether I shall complete this work. I shall speak perhaps more briefly of the remaining years. My strength is failing, and death is near.

The year of our Lord 1032: When my family arrived for their Michaelmas visit, they brought wheat, barley, onions, cabbage, and tallow. They did not bring my grandmother Bertha. She had died that summer. I was grieved.

The year of our Lord 1033: When my family arrived at Pentecost, Abbot Bern held a lengthy conference with my father and me. I was about to turn 20 years old. It was time for me either to leave the monastery and return to Altshausen, or to become a monk. I wanted more than anything to stay at the monastery as one of the brothers. I would not be able to keep the Rule of St. Benedict in every detail. I would be able to pray the hours, of course, and to engage in spiritual reading at the appointed hours. I had not the ability to take my turn in the kitchen, nor to perform five hours of manual labor each day. Abbot Bern said that, if I chose to stay, I could replace the manual labor with studies. I could think of nothing that would give me greater joy.

Abbot Bern required that I be served by brother monks and not by servants. Bertolf and Friderich were given the choice of staying and becoming monks themselves or returning to my father's house. Bertolf chose to go, and Friderich to stay. We were both received as novices on the Feast of Ss. Peter and Paul, after which my family and Bertolf left for Altshausen. As my care required two men, Berthold was appointed to take Bertolf's place.

The year of our Lord 1034: I received my black habit and became a Benedictine monk. In addition to my studies, I began to assist with the students at the cloister school. The younger ones would sit with me and turn the pages for me as I read. I would answer their questions. This practice allowed them to learn to understand my voice, which Abbot Bern considered important. It also allowed them to develop their skills in reading, as they followed along with me, and to learn about whatever subject I was reading.

The year of our Lord 1040: I completed the first draft of the Chronicle of the World, which collects all the important events from the birth of our Lord to our present day. When it was done, I sent it to St. Gallen's monastery, so the scholars there could check the dates against their records and provide corrections.

The year of our Lord 1043: Despite my infirmity, Abbot Bern insisted that I be ordained to the holy priesthood. I could not serve mass, of course, but I became the confessor for the students at the cloister school.

The year of our Lord 1048: Abbot Bern, our beloved father, died, and I was elected his successor. I sent a message to my family to let them know, and they came to the monastery to witness my receiving the abbatial blessing from the bishop.

The year of our Lord 1049: My sight had been failing for some time. In this year, I became entirely blind. This was not an entirely unwelcome development. The older students at the cloister school began to serve as my readers and scribes. This allowed them to understand the practical work involved in managing the abbey, and it allowed me better insight into their character and their needs. It also gave me more time to write poetry and hymns, which was, at this time, my greatest joy.

The year of our Lord 1052: My mother, Hiltrud, died in January. My father did not wait for the Pentecost visit but came immediately after her death. The world was cold. He came alone, to tell me of her death, and he asked me to write a verse for her tombstone.

Afterword from the monk Berthold: On the eve of the Feast of the Exaltation of the Holy Cross in the year 1054, Abbot Hermann, my beloved father and teacher and friend, fell asleep as he was telling his scribe of his mother's death. He slept serenely for a week. On his last day, he woke, made his confession, and received the Viaticum, then closed his eyes and passed into eternal life. After the funeral rites, we carried his body to Altshausen, where he was buried next to his mother.

Before his death, Abbot Hermann had asked me to judge whether this chronicle of his life was a worthy endeavor, and if it was, to transfer the text from the scribes' wax tablets to vellum. This was the most difficult task I have ever undertaken. Many days, I had to stop work lest my tears mar the page. Yet, at the same time, the work filled my heart with unspeakable joy.

When I started this task, I thought I might fill out the details of Abbot Hermann's life that he omitted, whether from modesty or from lack of strength as he neared the end of his life. He said nothing of his work creating astronomical instruments based on the Arabic documents that Abbot Bern had procured. The astrolabe and the quadrant were beautiful, but Abbot Hermann especially loved the portable sundial. Neither did he mention his work in music, nor the instructions he wrote on using an abacus, nor so many other things.

Yet it seems to me that I am not worthy to speak of those things of which he himself kept silent. I will therefore close this chronicle with the hymn that I love best of all the poems and hymns that Abbot Hermann wrote.

Loving mother of the Redeemer,
gate of heaven, star of the sea,
assist your people who have fallen yet strive to rise again.
To the wonderment of nature you bore your Creator,
yet remained a virgin after as before,
You who received Gabriel's joyful greeting,
have pity on us poor sinners.

St. Hermann of Reichenau

Although you will often find St. Hermann referred to as St. Hermann the Lame or St. Hermann the Cripple, he was, in his own time, known as Hermann, the Wonder of the Age.

Such a wonder he was! He was a poet, a hymnographer, and a scholar. The most important of his scholarly works was his *Chronicle of the World*. His scholarship, though, wasn't limited to history. It extended to astronomy, scientific instruments, music theory, and mathematics. He calculated the length of the lunar month and developed a new lunar calendar. He was interested, it seems, in everything, and he wrote about everything that interested him.

While he did insert events from his own life into the Chronicle of the World, including the birth of his brother Werner and the death of his mother, there is no evidence that he ever wrote a chronicle of his own life.

Since his death, those who have admired and venerated him have tried to understand what caused his condition. According to a 12th century English manuscript, he was attacked and mutilated by a bear. In more recent times, it has been suggested that he had a motor neuron disease such as amyotrophic lateral sclerosis or spinal muscular atrophy. I don't believe that we will ever have a clear diagnosis for St. Hermann's condition, and I don't believe that we need one.

Prayer
O God, who in your kindness called your servant Hermann to follow Christ, grant, we pray, through his intercession, that we may hold fast to you with all our heart. Through our Lord Jesus Christ, your Son, who lives and reigns with you in the unity of the Holy Spirit, one God, for ever and ever.

St. Gerald of Aurillac
Born around 855, Aurillac, France
Died around 909, Cézens, France

FEAST DAY OCTOBER 13

The new abbot stopped in the entry of the refectory. The mid-day meal was over, and the table servers and reader were taking their meal at the far end of the refectory. Two monks were gathering leftover food from the tables. One was tall and fair, neither young nor old, with red hair around his tonsure. The other was old. The wisps of hair around his tonsure were white, his skin weathered and brown. The abbot nodded to himself and made his way to the old monk.

"After you have taken the alms to the gate, Brother Hugh, come to my lodging," the abbot said in a low voice. The old monk, Brother Hugh, looked at him quizzically. "Brother Michiel can distribute the alms." Brother Hugh nodded and continued his work. The abbot turned and left.

Brother Hugh dumped bowls full of herring and onions into an iron pot. The berries and early plums had all been eaten, and the dishes of peppered venison and leeks had been scraped clean. Brother Michiel gathered the trenchers, thick slices of dark bread that served as plates for the monks. He carried them to the handcart sitting outside the door of the refectory and stacked them on a clean linen cloth that might once have been part of a tunic. Brother Hugh put the pots of herring next to the trenchers. Brother Michiel picked up the arms of the handcart and began pushing it towards the porch outside the abbey gate. The handcart squeaked and clanked. Brother Hugh walked in silence.

When they reached the porch, the poor of Tulle were already waiting. "I must go to the abbot," Brother Hugh said softly.

"I saw him speak to you," said Brother Michiel. "I will distribute the alms."

Brother Hugh nodded. Brother Michiel would share kindness and mercy with the food. Brother Hugh left the porch and walked to the abbot's lodging. A gray cat watched him go.

The afternoon was warm, and the shutters over the parlor windows were open. The parlor walls were covered in rich tapestries, and the rush mats on the floor were strewn with rosemary and mint. A light breeze came in through the windows, along with the murmuring of the abbey's chickens as they foraged in the yard.

"Please sit down," said Abbot Odo, gesturing towards the bench by the window. The bench was covered with silk cushions. Brother Hugh briefly considered removing the cushions, then changed his mind and sat where he was directed.

"I spent the last fortnight going through the abbey's records, Brother Hugh, and it appears that you have been here longer than anyone. Is that true?"

Brother Hugh thought for a moment. "I believe it is, my lord abbot," he said, without raising his eyes. "I came in the first year of the reign of King Odo, who was blessed to share your name. Many died of pestilence and flux that year and in the years that followed."

"The records say that many died, and that many left because they could not eat meat."

"That is true, my lord abbot. Brothers would feign illness that they might stay in the infirmary. There, they could sleep when it pleased them, and they had meals with meat thrice each day. Then pox came to the monastery, and many of these brothers regained their health that they might avoid the contagion. Some went on pilgrimages of thanksgiving and never returned, and some went back to their families. It was at this time that the abbot and the obedientiaries decided to allow meat in the refectory, so that our brothers could more readily maintain their vows of stability and obedience."

"I have observed that you eat not from the dish that contains meat."

"My lord abbot, that is so. The kitchen provides one dish with meat and one without, and I eat from the one without."

"Why is that?"

"When I served Count Gerald, the lord of Aurillac, he ate naught but fish and bread and vegetables, unless perchance he was sick. I followed his way of life as well as I could when I served him. When I came here, it was no hardship to continue."

Abbot Odo nodded. "I have also observed that the obedience of distributing the remains of our meals as alms to the poor is not shared among the brothers equally, but that you receive that obedience every week."

"Yes, my lord abbot. I learned to love almsgiving at the feet of my lord Gerald. When I shared with him my desire to live as he lived, he gave me leave to come here, where I might work and pray and serve the poor with fewer hindrances."

The two men sat for some time without speaking. The silence was filled with the humming of bees among the sunflowers outside the window and the distant chink-chink-chink of the blacksmith working at the forge.

At last the abbot spoke. "How is it that I know naught of Count Gerald? You speak of this lord almost as if he were a saint."

"My lord abbot, I am quite certain that he is a saint."

"Oh, Brother Hugh, lords and kings are not saints. They are strangers to God, cruel, violent, lecherous, greedy, and vain, entirely unfit for the Kingdom of Heaven."

"My lord Gerald was a pious man. He loved God and served the poor."

"Even if that were true, Brother Hugh, there are no more saints, no more miracles," said Abbot Odo, waving his hand as if he were batting away a fly. "We have reached the end of the age, and God will soon come to judge the living and the dead."

"Yet, my lord abbot, I have seen miracles."

Abbot Odo shook his head. "I have heard

stories of miracles, too, Brother Hugh. They are naught but travelers' tales and fables. God sent saints in times past, and those saints filled the world with signs and wonders. The world is no longer filled with wonders, Brother Hugh. It is filled with wars and rumors of wars, with famines and pestilences. Lawlessness abounds. These are the signs of the end of the age. There are no more miracles."

A hen cried out, warning of a hawk overhead.

"I am here, Brother Hugh," the abbot continued, "because men like your lord filled this abbey with their younger sons. Their sons accept the tonsure, but they refuse to keep silence, they refuse to work, they refuse to pray. They must have their meat at dinner, their riding cloaks lined with striped silk, their drawers of linen so fine and sheer that they might as well go without. Such men are not saints, Brother Hugh. Such men work no miracles."

"My lord abbot, my lord Gerald was a virgin. He had no sons. You must not blame him for the sons of other men."

Abbot Odo cleared his throat.

Brother Hugh blinked. "My lord abbot," he

said, "I speak with too much boldness. Forgive me."

Silence filled the parlor. Even the bees and the blacksmith made no sound. "God forgives, my son," Abbot Odo said at last. "That rebuke was well deserved."

Brother Hugh looked up. "My lord abbot?"

"If a good man strikes me, it is a kindness. If he rebukes me, it is chrism for my head." He took a deep breath. "I saw your piety, Brother Hugh, and I invited you to speak. Yet instead of listening to you, I silenced you." He shook his head. "God knows I am a fool, Brother Hugh. Now, please, tell me what you know of Count Gerald of Aurillac."

The chickens were once again murmuring in contentment.

"I met the lord Gerald when I came to his household as a page. My parents wanted me to be trained by a family who would teach me to pray as well as to fight, and they knew none other than my lord Gerald's parents who would do that. That is why my lord Gerald's own parents kept him after his childhood ended and trained him themselves."

"A moment please, Brother Hugh. Your

lord Gerald stayed with his parents, and was not fostered to another family?"

"Yes, my lord abbot. His parents, believing that their son had been born to them through divine providence, sought a family they could trust to train him in the fear of God. Not finding one, they continued his education themselves."

"I see. Pray, continue."

"My lord Gerald had but fourteen years when I came to his family, though he was tall for his age and well favored. His parents had engaged a tutor to teach him to read and to pray the Psalms, and another to teach him to play the lute and to sing. One of his father's men was training him in the arts related to warfare. His father was teaching him the skills required to oversee his estates and administer justice in his lands. My lord Gerald learned quickly, and he was becoming vain."

"As one might expect, when a child lives with his own parents for too long," said Abbot Odo.

"Even so," said Brother Hugh. "Yet God was with my lord Gerald, and sent him an affliction to cure his vanity and set him on a righteous path,"

"What was this affliction?" asked Abbot Odo.

"Pimples, my lord abbot."

Abbot Odo raised an eyebrow. "Pimples?"

"Yes, my lord abbot. He was covered from his scalp to his toes with fiery red pimples. His parents feared that their men would think he had a contagion and would flee, so they confined him to a room in the castle keep where he would not be seen. Their priest, Father Hildebart, prayed for my lord Gerald and anointed him with holy oil and gave him holy water to drink and had him bathe in water from a holy well. They called in doctors who smeared him with unguents and bled him until there was no color in his cheeks. His mother called for a wise woman who lived in the forest. Her remedies had no effect either. It seemed that he would always be covered in pimples.

"His parents knew that no army would follow a leader who was so disfigured, so they devised a new plan for his education. They would not train him to be a lord. Rather, Father Hildebart would train him to be a leader in the church. Perhaps an abbot like yourself."

Abbot Odo nodded. A shepherd's dog

barked somewhere in the distance. Abbot Odo motioned for Hugh to continue.

"My lord Gerald loved his new course of learning," Brother Hugh said, "even more than he had loved hawks and hounds. Under Father Hildebart's guidance, my lord Gerald began to see the wickedness of his vanity. When he confessed this most grievous sin with tears and true repentance, the pimples were healed."

"Think you then that God sent the pimples and took them away?" asked Abbot Odo.

"Indeed, my lord abbot," said Brother Hugh.

The sound of the church bells broke the quiet. Abbot Odo and Brother Hugh stood. "What obedience is yours to fulfill after the prayers of the ninth hour?" Abbot Odo asked as they made their way to the church.

"There are some who abide outside our walls who lack the strength to come to the abbey to receive alms. Brother Michiel and I take surplus food from the kitchens to their homes on Wednesdays."

"After you complete your work of mercy, if there be time before vespers, return to my lodging," Abbot Odo said. "I would learn more of your lord Gerald."

"Yes, my lord abbot." They entered the church together and went to their places. Two monks slipped into the church from the night stairs as the chanting began.

"How long is it until vespers?" Brother Hugh asked Brother Michiel as they entered the monastery gate.

Brother Michiel set down the handles of the empty handcart and looked towards the sun. "A half an hour, I think. Perhaps more if the sacristan be sleeping."

"I must return to the abbot's lodging. He has asked me to teach him what I know of the lord Gerald."

"Give me that basket and be on your way," said Brother Michiel. "Tell the abbot, if you will, that I was the first person healed by the lord Gerald's wash water."

Brother Hugh stopped. "Brother Michiel, how long have I known you, and you have not told me this?"

"It is ten years since I joined the abbey."

"For ten years you have known me and yet spoke not of this?"

"For ten years, you asked me not what I knew of the lord Gerald. Now go to the abbot, my brother."

Brother Hugh pushed the empty basket into Brother Michiel's hands. "I go," he said. He walked to the cloister to wash his hands in the long marble basin, then to the abbot's lodging. The abbot's door was standing open.

"Welcome, Brother Hugh," Abbot Odo said from within. "Come in, take your seat, and speak to me of Count Gerald."

Brother Hugh entered, eyes cast down.

"You told me earlier that your lord Gerald was a virgin," the abbot said. "Are you certain of that? Could it have pleased him to take a woman in a secret place, where she had no one to defend her? Or could he have been born a eunuch?"

"He was not a eunuch, my lord abbot. It was not out of any lack of virility, but out of love for the beauty of virginity and fear of the fires of hell that he made a vow of chastity when he was still a youth. Only once came he near to breaking this vow."

"Tell me of it," said Abbot Odo.

"The year my lord Gerald came of age, a pestilence swept the land and took both his parents, and he became the lord of all his parents' lands and people. He wanted to flee to a monastery, but the weight of his duties constrained him. He began to spend his days walking about his estates, asking God and the saints to guide him. One day, he saw a maiden, a serf, who was of surpassing beauty. He wanted to take her, but, mindful of his vow, he fled back to the castle keep and spent the rest of the day in the oratory, asking God to preserve him from sin.

"Yet that night he could think of nothing but the maiden. The next morning, he sent a message to her father, instructing him to bring her to a secret place that night. Her father brought her, and when my lord Gerald took her to the chamber he had prepared, she would neither look at him nor touch him. Filled with shame, my lord Gerald fled back to his chambers. He called for Father Hildebart and made a full confession that very night.

"As penance, Father Hildebart required him to give the maiden her liberty and a small holding and to command her father to give her in marriage to an honorable and free man of his choosing. My lord Gerald went himself to her father the very next day. Having thus paid his debt to her, my lord Gerald returned to Father Hildebart and made anew his vow of chastity, this time with a witness."

Brother Hugh stopped speaking to collect his thoughts. It had been years since he had said so many words in so little time. Abbot Odo shared his silence. In the distance, the goatherd sang, calling the goats back to their enclosure for milking.

"God accepted the vow," Brother Hugh continued, "and in his love and mercy, he struck my lord Gerald with blindness, to prevent him from looking at a woman with lust."

"God thought it too much to ask him to pluck out his own eyes?"

"It may be so, my lord abbot. My lord Gerald thought it better to lose his sight than to be thrown into hell. At the same time, his men thought that if the neighboring lords learned that he was blind, they would have laid siege to the castle, killed my lord Gerald, and taken his lands. We all worked diligently to ensure that no one might learn of his blindness. For his part, my lord Gerald knew that God chastises those he loves, and he waited patiently for God to restore his sight."

"How long was he blind, Brother Hugh?" asked Abbot Odo.

"A little more than a year, my lord abbot."

"You are certain that he never had a woman after the blindness?"

"I am sure, my lord abbot. His purity was such that he bade me prepare a basin and clean night clothes for him each evening before he slept, so that he might have the means to remove the uncleanness should he be polluted in his sleep."

Abbot Odo frowned. "Were these nighttime pollutions not a sign that his daytime thoughts were filled with lust?"

"No, my lord abbot. Father Hildebart determined that they were neither from lust, nor from gluttony, but like the lice and worms that afflicted him, they were the natural release of an excess of humors."

"Say you that God sent the blindness and the pimples to Count Gerald for his salvation?"

"Yes, my lord abbot."

"What of the night pollutions?"

"God sent them to be a thorn in my lord Gerald's flesh, that he might not think himself better than other men."

"It may be so. Yet if the illnesses and healings were miracles, it seems that God sent them out of His abundant mercy, as he sends the rain on the just and the unjust alike. They are not signs that Count Gerald was a saint."

The bells for vespers began to ring. From the steps outside abbot's lodging, the gray cat watched Abbot Odo and Brother Hugh walk in silence towards the church. Abbot Odo paused at the door. "Please return to my quarters after the ninth hour tomorrow," he said.

"Forgive me, my lord abbot, I cannot. Tomorrow is Thursday. Brother Michiel and I will be washing the feet of the poor."

"Then I will join you and Brother Michiel."

Early Thursday morning, Brother Hugh stood in the dim light of the almonry, the small building near the monastery gate where alms were stored. He looked over the shelves, picking out tunics, hose, shoes, and other items that they might give the poor who had need of them. He stacked them carefully next to the basins and towels and a basket of soap. He had just opened a locked chest and taken out a box of coins when the squeaking song of the handcart announced the arrival of Abbot Odo and Brother Michiel.

The gray cat watched as Brother Hugh carried the basins, towels, and soap to the cart, then went back inside the almonry. Abbot Odo picked up a bar of soap and sniffed it. "Why is it, Brother Michiel," asked the abbot, "that we have this fine soap from Aleppo? Can we not make soap ourselves?"

"The mother of one of our brothers provides it for the abbey," said Brother Michiel. Abbot Odo looked at him curiously. Brother Michiel shrugged. "She says her son's skin is too delicate for ordinary soap."

Brother Hugh returned with the coins and the clothing and added them to the cart. Brother Michiel took up the arms of the cart and pulled it from the almonry through the gate to the porch. Brother Hugh and Abbot Odo walked beside him.

The porter had set up benches on the porch enough to seat 12 men. Brother Hugh looked over the men who were waiting. "Where is Bernart Fuller?" he asked.

"Goody Fuller has a fever," Gilebert Tanner replied. "He stays by her side and refuses to leave."

"The leech says this illness will be unto her death," said Ewart.

"Gilebert and Ewart, sit you down in the middle of the bench," said Brother Hugh. "You others, fill in on either side. Ewart, has the fever struck anyone else in the fuller's household?"

"No, Brother Hugh. Nor any of the neighbors neither."

When the first 12 men had taken their places on the bench, Abbot Odo blessed them, then knelt in front of the man on the left end of the bench. The man squinted at him. "Be you the abbot?" the man asked.

"Indeed I am," said Abbot Odo. "Who are you?"

"I be the cesspit worker, my lord abbot."

"Have you a name?"

"None that anyone know," he said.

Brother Hugh walked up, carrying a basin of water. "My lord abbot," he said quietly.

Abbot Odo turned, then motioned to the

ground in front of the cesspit worker. Brother Hugh set the basin at the place the abbot indicated, then handed him the towel and soap that he had tucked inside the fold of his scapular. Abbot Odo turned back to the cesspit worker. "Had your parents a name for you?" he asked as he gently removed the man's shoes. Brother Hugh noted that the man had no hose, and half the sole of the left shoe was missing. He went back to the cart.

The man shook his head. "They died when I were a child."

"Can you tell me about them?" Abbot Odo asked as he began carefully washing the man's feet.

The man smiled wistfully. "My mother, she was a serf. She belonged to a lord in Aurillac," he said. "The lord, he gave her freedom and a piece of land at the edge of his domain, and she was married to a freeman that were in his service. My father, he took me up to the castle to visit from time to time. It was always quiet and peaceful, like a church almost. The lord, he never allowed no drunkenness nor nothing like that."

Abbot Odo nodded as he inspected a wound on the cesspit cleaner's foot. It was beginning to fester. He made a note to have the infirmarer visit him before the wound turned gangrenous.

"How came you here?" asked Abbot Odo.

The cesspit cleaner closed his eyes and frowned. He shook his head. "My parents, they was gentle and meek," he said. "Some soldiers, they came, and they killed my parents and burned their house and took me away. My mother, when she was dying, she told me never to tell no one my name, because it might be worse for me if the soldiers knew." He sighed. "There be no soldiers here, though, and you be an abbot. My mother, I think she would let me tell an abbot. They called me Gerald, after the lord of Aurillac."

Abbot Odo looked up into the eyes of the man in front of him. Gerald, after the lord of Aurillac. Yes, that's what the man had said. He dried Gerald's feet, careful not to touch the festering wound. "May our gracious Lord guide the steps of the servant of God Gerald, and lead him on a level path," he said, kissing Gerald's feet. As Abbot Odo moved to the next man, Gerald rose.

"Sit you down," Brother Hugh said gently. He knelt before the cesspit cleaner, hose and shoes from the cart in his hands. He pulled the hose over the man's feet, tying them below the knee. He put the shoes on his feet, then gave him a coin. Standing and giving him his hand, he said, "Rise now my brother."

Gerald stood, then bowed first to Brother Hugh and then to Abbot Odo, who was already taking off the shoes of the next man on the bench. Gerald moved away, and another took his place.

When all the feet had been washed and kissed, and clothes and coins distributed, Brother Hugh and Brother Michiel loaded the basins and towels into the hand cart. "Brother Michiel," said Abbot Odo, "I was told that you have washed the feet of the poor every week since you came to the monastery. Is that true?"

"No, my lord abbot," Brother Michiel replied, taking up the handles of the cart. "When I first came, it was Brother Hugh's obedience to wash the feet of the poor, and a different brother joined him each week." He began pulling the cart toward the almonry. Abbot Odo walked beside him.

"Is the cesspit cleaner often among the poor you serve?" Abbot Odo asked.

"Always, my lord abbot," said Brother

Michiel.

"Know you of his history?"

"He says naught of himself, my lord abbot, and we ask naught."

Abbot Odo frowned. "How came you to receive this obedience every week, Brother Michiel?"

"I asked for the blessing," said Brother Michiel.

"Why is that?"

"I was born lame, and my parents gave me to the village smith to work the bellows, so that I might not have to beg. God spoke to the smith in a dream, telling him that I would be healed if he washed my legs and feet with water in which Count Gerald, the lord of Aurillac, had washed his hands."

Odo stopped walking. "He washed you thus?"

"Yes, my lord abbot," said Brother Michiel, standing in the gate. "Lord Gerald told the smith that the dream was a delusion and sent him away. The smith, though, he knew the voice of God, so he went to the kitchen and asked a maid if she would give him a jug of water in which the lord had washed his hands. She gave it, and when the smith washed my legs and feet, I was healed."

"I knew of that miracle," said Brother Hugh, "although I learned only yesterday that the smith's boy was Brother Michiel."

The abbot looked from Brother Michiel to Brother Hugh. "You told me not of this miracle," he said.

"Forgive me, my lord abbot. Yet I told you that I had seen miracles."

"Indeed. You told me that God twice afflicted Count Gerald in his flesh to preserve him from sin, and twice healed him. Were there other miracles?"

"There were many, my lord abbot," said Brother Michiel. "When people learned that God would heal through the lord Gerald's wash water, as He had healed through the napkins of St. Paul and the shadow of St. Peter, crowds began to come to the castle to beg for the miraculous water, and many were healed."

"It was so," said Brother Hugh. "Yet the healings filled lord Gerald with fury. Although he never maimed a thief, or a runaway serf, or an enemy caught in battle, he threatened to maim all his household if they continued to give his wash water to heal the sick."

Abbot Odo shook his head. "What you say makes no sense."

"It was the fear of God, my lord abbot. He was afraid that the gift of healing would cause him to be proud, and he would have to beseech God to afflict him again in his flesh so that he might not be cast into hell."

"No, I understand that," said Abbot Odo. "You said he never maimed anyone. Yet it was his duty to protect his borders and administer justice over his lands."

"Indeed, my lord abbot. His people oft complained that his justice was too mild, and that he showed too much mercy. There was the incident when a serving man entered his chamber to steal a red silk pillow. Lord Gerald gave him the pillow, along with a jeweled brooch, and suggested where he might sell them without risk." Abbot Odo snorted. "Believe me, my lord abbot. It is true, and not only with offenses against his person. Neighboring lords would bring armies into his land and attack the serfs and freemen, then flee when the lord Gerald came against them. They knew that if he captured them, he would simply admonish them and send them away."

Abbot Odo closed his eyes, trying to make sense of the cesspit worker and his parents and a lord with healing in his hands, hands that failed to defend his lands and goods. He gave up. Opening his eyes, he said, "Let us finish our work and go to vespers."

"As you will," said Brother Michiel, and he began pulling the cart towards the almonry. The chickens, annoyed by the sound of the cart, moved out of his way.

On Friday morning, Brother Michiel and Brother Hugh were the last of the brethren to leave the chapter house. The air was cool and fresh; the sun was just barely over the horizon. Brother Michiel and Brother Hugh were assigned to harvest peas.

They went to the barn to get baskets, then down the path to the pea field. Abbot Odo was there before them.

"Will you be gathering peas with us this fine morning?" asked Brother Michiel.

"I will," said Abbot Odo. "I dreamed of your lord Gerald last night. If you are willing to talk as we work, perhaps you can speak to me of him."

"I am willing," said Brother Michiel.

"As am I," said Brother Hugh.

Birds flitted in and out of the hedge, chittering and twittering and calling to each other. Beyond the hedge, Brother Hugh put baskets ahead of them in the rows, and the three men started to work.

"I had thought I would have you tell me of other miracles that your lord Gerald worked," said Abbot Odo, pulling pea pods from the plants and tossing them in his basket. "In my dream, though, it seemed that Count Gerald told me that the miracles he worked were not intended as a sign for me. He said that if the stories of all his miracles were told to me and confirmed by witnesses, I would say that his miracles proved nothing. The servants of Pharoah could do miracles as well as Moses, and those miracles were confirmed by the Holy Scriptures themselves."

"Lord Gerald would speak thus," said Brother Hugh.

"He spoke truth," said Abbot Odo. "He told me that I should inquire, not of his miracles, but of his mercy and his charity." Abbot Odo checked the plant carefully to ensure he'd gotten all the peas, then moved on. "Brother Michiel, what can you tell me of those things?"

Brother Michiel passed by several small pods that could wait to be picked another day. "The lord Gerald was known for his kindness to the poor. In his great hall, he had tables set up for the poor. As many as fifty ate in the hall with him, twice each day, although he ate but once. The poor were not given the trenchers and the remains from the high tables after the great people ate. They ate the same food as the members of his household, at the same time, in the same room."

Abbot Odo raised his brows, then looked to Brother Hugh. "Is that true?"

"It is, my lord abbot," said Brother Hugh. As he reached for a pod, a mouse darted from under the plant and scrambled down the row and out of sight. The gray cat raced after it.

"That seems excessive," said the abbot. "Almost womanly."

"Indeed, that was sometimes said of him," said Brother Hugh. "People also spoke of his reluctance to fight and kill as weak and womanly. He said that every man is made in the image of the Lord Christ, and he would not defile his sword by spilling their blood. When he could refuse a fight without dishonor, he refused. When he was compelled to fight, he commanded his men to fight with the flat of their swords and the butt of their spears."

"That sounds like the sort of tale that is told around a fire when the sky is dark and much ale has been drunk."

"Yet it is true, my lord abbot," said Brother Hugh "I was there when the lord Gerald gave these commands."

"Why would his men follow him, then? Could they not find a better master?"

"Because, my lord abbot, the lord Gerald never lost a battle."

"That is true," said Brother Michiel. "Everyone in the surrounding country knew it. When his men fought as the lord Gerald commanded them, they could not lose."

Abbot Odo picked up his basket and moved it farther down the row. "So Count Gerald achieved his victories without killing anyone, and without maiming those he captured."

"That is so," said Brother Hugh. "Out of reverence for the Lord Christ, in whose image they were made, he would not maim his captives. Once or twice, his men maimed prisoners before they brought them to the lord Gerald, knowing that he would not do it."

"What punishments gave he when his men defied him?"

"For this offense, my lord abbot, he gave no punishment. He understood his men's weakness, and he chose to teach them by exhortation and example rather than punishment."

"Your lord Gerald was not like other men," said Abbot Odo.

"He was not," said Brother Michiel.

"He was a saint," said Brother Hugh.

The gray cat sat in front of the abbot's basket and began washing its back legs. The men continued their work without speaking. They moved the full baskets to the edge of the field and began filling the next baskets. The sun moved higher. The clear sky was the same brilliant blue as Our Lady's robes in the church.

After a time, Brother Michiel spoke. "Are you certain it was the lord Gerald in your dream?"

"The man in my dream said it was he," said Abbot Odo. "Yet I am not certain. It could be that he was naught but a fantasy, or perchance even a demon sent to deceive."

They continued working their way down the last rows of peas. When they finished, the cat had disappeared.

Brother Michiel checked the position of the sun. "We have time to wash and to shave before Terce," he said.

"We would not have finished the harvest this morning without your help, my lord abbot," said Brother Hugh. "Thank you."

"Thanks be to God," said Abbot Odo.

The next day at chapter, Abbot Odo announced that he would be away for some weeks, fulfilling his abbatial duties at Cluny and other nearby monasteries. He did not mention that he would also be visiting Aurillac, where he hoped to talk with Father Hildebart and others who might have known Count Gerald, to learn from them the manner and quality of his life. While he was gone, Prior Gefrei would preside at the morning chapter meetings, at prayers, and at the mass.

During the first week Abbot Odo was away, Brother Hugh and Brother Michiel weeded the vegetable gardens and the lentil fields and gathered plums and berries. They swept the mats on the floor of the dormitory and replaced the withered mint with fresh lavender, and they gathered herbs to be dried for the winter. They distributed alms, and when they washed the feet of the poor, they rejoiced to learn that the fuller's wife had survived her illness. Brother Michiel mended cowls and tunics that were destined for the almonry. Brother Hugh returned a volume of hymns to the library and took out a collection of the writings of St. Basil the Great. The text was large and clear, and Brother Hugh found himself wondering if the scribe who had made the copy had eyes as old and weak as his.

During the second week Abbot Odo was away, the number of monks reporting to the infirmary increased. There were no fevers, no flux, only great weakness and a persistent, dry cough. Instead of beef, the sick were served poached eggs, pigeon stew with figs and raisins, and rosemary chamomile tea.

By the third week Abbot Odo was away, the number of the sick had increased until additional monks had to be assigned to minister to the sick according to the Rule. The outbreak lasted another three weeks, until Abbot Odo's return.

The abbot spent his first week back dealing with administrative matters that had accumulated in his absence and conferring with Prior Gefrei and the obedientiaries. After receiving the infirmarer's report, he found himself thinking that some of the brothers would benefit from more severe penances for idleness and deceit. As he considered that, he thought a voice whispered, "exhortation and example, my lord abbot."

At chapter on Monday, Abbot Odo was assigned to work with three of the boys of the abbey to clean out the chicken coop, scrub it inside and out, and provide it with fresh bedding. Prior Gefrei was assigned to work in the scullery. Brother Hugh noticed raised eyebrows here and there around the chapter house, but no one said anything.

The next day Prior Gefrei joined the brothers hauling charcoal from the kiln in the forest to the storage shed by the smithy. Abbot Odo assisted with the laundry for the infirmary.

It was the same the next day, and the next, and the next, until there were no longer raised eyebrows. The prior and the abbot might spend their afternoon work time on administrative tasks, but every morning, they took on the least-favored labors of their brothers.

When the morning labors were done, they invited the brothers they had worked with to join them at their table for the mid-day meal. There was no meat at the abbot's table, yet no one turned down the invitation, and when Brother Michiel and Brother Hugh cleared the tables, the serving dishes at the abbot's table had been scraped clean.

On a bright, clear morning, Brother Michiel, Brother Hugh, and Abbot Odo were assigned to clean the abbot's lodging. They left the chapter house together. "Have you rue and wormwood you can bring?" asked Abbot Odo. "The fleas have been terrible."

"No, my lord abbot," said Brother Hugh. "We can gather some later today, though, after the sun has dried the herbs and after we have cleaned the floors."

The gray cat followed the men into the

abbot's lodging. Abbot Odo opened the shutters in the parlor, and the cat jumped up on the window ledge. Abbot Odo looked at the floors. "I think the first thing to do is to take up the rush mats and put them in the sun to drive out the fleas."

As Brother Hugh and Brother Michiel took up the mats in the hall and parlor, Abbot Odo took up the mats in his bedchamber. "The cushions can go out in the sun as well," he said. The gray cat followed them as they carried mats and cushions outside. She sniffed the mats, then turned and settled herself on a cushion.

As they went back inside, Abbot Odo took up the broom. "If it pleases you to talk as we work," he said, "I have some questions for you."

"What are they, my lord abbot?" asked Brother Hugh.

"Know you a man named Witard? He is a well-born layman, once a knight in the army of Gerald of Aurillac."

"Know him?" Brother Hugh smiled broadly. "When we campaigned with Duke William, Witard taught me how to prepare my lord Gerald's arms and armor for combat."

"So you fought with Gerald then?"

"I went with him, yes, when Duke William commanded his service."

Abbot Odo stopped sweeping and leaned on his broom "What was the cause of battle?"

"Count Ademar and his allies had been harassing serfs and freemen who had no arms and no means to defend themselves, and Duke William believed that he and my lord Gerald could drive them away, so that the poor could live in peace."

"So also that Count Gerald and Duke William would have Count Ademar's land?"

"No, my lord abbot. They sought nothing beyond what God had already given them. They wanted only to protect the weak, as God gave them strength."

Brother Michiel looked around the room. "I'll fetch a bucket of water and soap for the floors," he said. Abbot Odo nodded his assent.

"Tell me about this campaign," said Abbot Odo.

"Give me the broom, my lord abbot, and I shall sweep as I talk."

Abbot Odo handed him the broom, then looked around his lodging. "It has been too long since I cleaned my own chambers," he said. He opened a cabinet, got a woolen cloth, and began wiping down the benches and tables. "I will listen as we work."

"Before the campaign, my lord Gerald told his knights that they were to take no spoils from the villeins or serfs. If they needed anything that was not provided for them, they were free to buy it at a fair price, and he distributed coins to all his men for that purpose."

"Lords and kings have the right to take what they need. Why did he forgo that right?"

"Because we were going to war to protect the poor from those who would despoil their homes and their holdings. My lord Gerald was certain that God would remove His protection from him and his army if they became the despoilers themselves."

"Would his men accept this command?" Abbot Odo asked.

"Yes, my lord abbot. They trusted that God would protect them if they obeyed lord Gerald."

Brother Michiel came back inside and set a bucket on the floor. He pulled a bar of soap from the fold in his scapular, took out his knife, and began shaving soap into the water. Abbot Odo and Brother Hugh sat at the table and began wiping down candlesticks and polishing silver.

"Those in the towns and the fields also knew that the lord Gerald and his men were no danger to them," Brother Hugh continued, "and that could turn the tide of a battle."

"How so?" asked Abbot Odo. "How could men without weapons or knowledge of the art of war make a difference?"

"Men without weapons, and women too, have eyes to see, my lord abbot, and ears to hear, and tongues to speak," said Brother Michiel. "Have you a brush for scrubbing the floor?"

"In the cabinet there," Abbot Odo replied, then turned to Brother Hugh. "What of Duke William? Gave he the same orders to his men?"

"No, my lord abbot," said Brother Hugh. "There was some murmuring among my lord Gerald's men, yet none of them died, and few were injured. That was not so with Duke William's men."

"So the campaign ended, and Count Gerald had the victory."

"It was not as simple as that, my lord abbot.

When my lord Gerald returned to his castle, he found that it had been taken by a small company of Count Ademar's men. All of his own people who had survived the attack were sheltering in the keep, and Count Ademar's men controlled the bailey. So my lord Gerald laid siege to his own castle."

"How long was the siege?"

"It lasted but two days, my lord abbot. The larger part of Count Ademar's army was on the way to reinforce the company inside the castle and had camped for the night not far from the castle. They sent scouts ahead to ascertain the lord Gerald's position, and the scouts encountered an old woman carrying wood from the forest. She warned them that she had seen an army large and fierce, and persuaded them that the rocky outcroppings they could see in the distance were the tents and pavilions of this army. They returned to Count Ademar, and she found my lord Gerald and reported what she had seen and heard. The next morning, after ascertaining that Count Ademar and his army had departed, my lord Gerald sent a knight to parley with the men in the bailey. The knight told them that their lord had fled, and if they laid down their arms and opened the gates, the lord Gerald would allow them to leave."

"Without ransom?"

"Indeed," said Brother Hugh. "After they left, my lord Gerald and his men buried those who had been killed when the castle was taken, whom Count Ademar's men had left unburied."

"When I was in Aurillac," said Abbot Odo, "I met Count Ademar." The gray cat jumped up into the window. The abbot went on. "He said he had once been an enemy of the lord Gerald, and an enemy of the monastery at Tulle. When he failed to take the lord Gerald's castle and lands, he turned on this monastery in his wrath, and stole all that he could carry. He's old now, and the lord Gerald has been coming to him in his dreams. He made a pilgrimage to Aurillac to venerate the lord Gerald's tomb and to seek his forgiveness. He said he will come here just after the feast of St. Denis to make recompense for the stolen treasure and to seek forgiveness here."

"My lord Gerald died just after the feast of St. Denis," said Brother Hugh.

"Has your lord Gerald the ability to influence men of wealth and power, to lead them to God?" Abbot Odo asked.

"If he had not that ability, Brother Hugh would not be standing here," said Brother

Michiel. "You, also, my lord abbot. Has my lord Gerald not influenced you?"

Abbot Odo closed his eyes, thinking. "He has," he said at last. "He has. Yet I gave up my wealth and power to become a monk. I left the world to enter God's kingdom. Brother Hugh also left the world, and you as well, Brother Michiel. Your lord Gerald, though, never left the world. How is it possible that a man who kept his wealth, who led armies, who exercised power in the world, how is it possible for such a man to be a saint?"

"Was not King David a man after God's own heart?" asked Brother Hugh.

"He was," said Abbot Odo. "Even so, our Lord said that it is harder for a camel to go through the eye of a needle." He stopped, shaking his head.

"Than for a rich man to enter the Kingdom of Heaven," said Brother Hugh. "Yet with God, all things are possible. Even this."

St. Gerald of Aurillac

In Gaul, in the ninth century, many people believed that the end of the world was at hand. The Christian lands were being attacked by Vikings and Magyars and Muslims. Powerful men treated churches and monasteries as their private possessions. They had their younger sons made monks to keep them out of the way unless they were needed. The younger sons expected to be treated like little lords in the monastery, with all the luxuries to which they were accustomed.

When St. Odo became the second abbot of Cluny, he took on the task of reforming the spiritual lives of the monasteries and restoring them to the Rule of St. Benedict. If he hadn't already been convinced that rich and powerful men couldn't be saints, the difficulties he faced in this work would have persuaded him.

By the time he wrote *The Life of St. Gerald of Aurillac*, though, Odo believed that Gerald was a saint. He didn't come to that conclusion easily. He investigated Gerald's life thoroughly, interviewing "the monk Hugh, the priest Hildebart, and two well-born laymen, Witard and another Hildebart, along with many others," sometimes alone and sometimes together. Stories that he must have considered absurd when he first heard them, like Gerald commanding his men to fight with the flats of their swords, Odo confirmed in his research.

Odo clearly expected others to have the same reservations he did. He wrote Gerald's *Life* in large part to justify the idea that it was possible for a man like Gerald, a man of wealth and power, to be a saint.

Prayer
Lord God, You alone are holy and no one is good without You. Through the intercession of St. Gerald, help us to live in such a way that we may not be deprived of a share in Your glory. Amen.

St. Angadrisma of Beauvais
Born c. 615, Thérouanne, Neustria, Kingdom of the Franks
Died c. 695, Beauvais, Neustria, Kingdom of the Franks

FEAST DAY OCTOBER 14

Berevera stood just inside the stable door. She waited a moment for her eyes to adjust to the dim light. "Angadrisma!" she called softly. "Angadrisma, are you here? Dame Wulfgurd requires you."

Angadrisma patted the black mare's nose one more time, then slipped out of her stall, latching the stall door carefully behind her. "I am here," she said. "Where is Grandmama?"

"Come with me," Berevera said. "I will take you to her."

"You won't tell her that I was in the stables, will you?" asked Angadrisma.

"She knows," said Berevera.

Dame Wulfgurd was sitting on a stone bench under an ancient oak tree, spinning fine woolen thread. Her distaff was fastened in her belt behind her. Her tunic was woven of silk and wool, dark green with gold and russet trim, and it shimmered in the morning sunlight.

She looked up when Berevera and Angadrisma approached and set her spindle in the fiber on her distaff. "See to it that we are not disturbed," said Dame Wulfgurd to Berevera.

"Yes, Madam," said Berevera.

Angadrisma approached her grandmother cautiously. She knelt and kissed her hand, then rose and kissed her cheek. "I am here, Grandmama," she said.

"You were in Lord Egric's stables," Dame Wulfgurd said.

Angadrisma's eyes lit up. "Yes, Grandmama! I went to see the black mare. Have you seen her? The stablehands call her the death horse, but she is beautiful! She has not a single white hair on her, but is all black and shining. I brought her an apple, to make friends with her."

"Stop, Angadrisma," Dame Wulfgurd said. "I did not summon you here to discuss horses."

"But Grandmama ..."

"We have been at Lord Egric's manor but two days, and already you are disobeying your father. Have you forgotten his command that you must not enter the stables alone?"

"No, Grandmama, I have not forgotten, but I was not alone. Lord Egric's stablehands were there, and some of King Dagobert's men."

"Angadrisma."

"Yes, Grandmama?"

Dame Wulfgurd sighed deeply. "Angadrisma, our lord Dagobert's men are exactly the reason you must not be in the stables without me or your father."

"But Grandmama—"

"Angadrisma, listen to me. I do not trust the king's men. Not with you. You are beautiful, Angadrisma, like your mother was. I see how the men look at you."

"I don't understand, Grandmama."

Dame Wulfgurd took Angadrisma's face in her hands. "If one of the king's men sees you in a private place, Angadrisma, and loves the bud more than the blossom, he could take you, and before you could scream or run away, he would deflower you, and have you as his wife."

Angadrisma raised her head ever so

slightly. "No man can have me as a wife, Grandmama. I am not yet twelve years old."

"It does not matter, Angadrisma. Such men care little about age, and nothing at all for the wives and concubines they already have. They would see your beauty, and look on you with lust, and that would be that."

"Papa would have them killed!"

"And if he did, what would become of you? No other man would have you as a wife, no nunnery would take you. You could be a concubine, perhaps, and the wives would hate you, and your children would war with their children. No, Angadrisma, your father would not have them killed. He would have you marry the man."

"But—"

"Enough, Angadrisma! I had planned to give you Berevera on your twelfth birthday. I see now that I cannot wait until you come of age. You will have her now. She will attend you and accompany you wherever you go. You will not be without her. Do you understand me?"

"Yes, Grandmama."

"Go to the parlor now. I will send Berevera

to you there. She will get the lice out of your hair and the muck off your shoes before you come to dinner."

"Yes, Grandmama," said Angadrisma. She knelt and kissed her grandmother's hand, then stood and kissed her cheek. Dame Wulfgurd took her spindle from the distaff and resumed spinning.

The hall smelled of roast chickens and the stew that was bubbling in the great iron cauldron over the fire. Servants were everywhere, setting up benches and spreading white linen cloths on the tables for dinner. A manservant was on the dais, unfolding King Dagobert's throne. Trying to stay out of everyone's way, Angadrisma walked along the wall and across the dais, then through the drapes that separated the parlor from the rest of the hall. No one else was in the parlor. She sat on a chest and waited for Berevera.

As she waited, she looked at the pattern that was woven into the red wool curtains that surrounded Lord Egric's bed. The same pattern, of horses and birds, vines and trees, was carved into the posts that held up the walls of the hall and embroidered around the edges of the parlor drapes.

Berevera came through the drapes. "Look, Berevera!" said Angadrisma. "Look at the drapes and the posts and the curtains! They all have horses!"

"Hmm," said Berevera. She opened a chest and pulled out a fine-toothed comb and a jar of thick ointment made from beeswax, pork grease, and lavender. "Now, child, sit you here in the light, and turn around." She dipped the comb into the ointment, then began carefully combing Angadrisma's hair.

Angadrisma was still asleep on her featherbed, tucked under a bench at the side of the parlor, when one of the menservants picked up the bench and moved it to the dais.

"Come, Angadrisma, wake up," said Berevera. "We need to get you dressed for Mass."

Angadrisma yawned, then sat up. Her father, Lord Radobertus, was already up and dressed in his blue silk tunic, which set off the reddish gold of his braids and beard. King Dagobert was resplendent in a purple tunic, his dark hair flowing down his back almost to his knees.

"Where is Grandmama?" she asked

Berevera.

"She is on her way to the chapel with the king's wives. Now, would you wear your green silk tunic today?"

"Yes, Berevera."

Berevera pulled the tunic over Angadrisma's undergown and fastened a woven belt around her waist. "Now sit you here while I dress your hair."

"Yes, Berevera."

Lord Radobertus opened a chest, pulled out a stack of documents tied together with a red ribbon, and stood up. He nodded approvingly at Angadrisma. "As soon as Berevera finishes with you, you must head to the chapel for Mass. I will not be there today. The king and Lord Egric require my presence. When Mass is over, you may return here or walk through the gardens. Berevera will stay with you. You may not visit the stables. Do you have any questions?"

"No, Papa." He stepped towards her and held out his hand. She kissed it. He knelt so she could kiss his cheek, then he stood and went through the curtain to the dais.

If King Dagobert had been at Mass that day, perhaps the priest would have preached a different homily. The king was not there, though, and the priest took advantage of the opportunity to deplore lust and lechery, and to praise the beauty of monogamy and the even greater beauty of virginity. His voice rose and fell like the currents in a river. His words filled Angadrisma's heart, and she felt something like desire rise in her. When the service was over, she turned to Berevera. "I will speak to the priest," she whispered.

Berevera nodded and walked to the chapel door, where she waited in silence.

The priest consumed the last of the Holy Gifts, finished his prayers, then began putting out the lamps around the nave. He noticed a maiden standing near the steps to the altar. She neither moved nor spoke.

"My daughter," he said as he worked, "would you speak with me?"

"I would," she answered.

He stepped to the next lamp without turning towards her. "Then speak."

"Can a woman who is not a nun make a vow of virginity?"

The priest stopped and turned to look at the maiden. Her eyes were gray, and her long hair was the color of sunlight. Her skin was as smooth as the silk she wore. With both beauty and wealth, she was a maiden that men would willingly fight and kill for. He considered her question. Finally, he spoke. "Do you wish to make such a vow?"

"I –" the maiden began, then said no more. She seemed to the priest like a wild animal that would flee at any sudden movement.

"I will not tell anyone what you say to me here," the priest said.

The maiden looked at the floor. "My grandmother tells me that I am beautiful, but you have made me see that my beauty is nothing compared to the beauty of the Mother of God and the holy virgins." She paused and took a deep breath. Her hands were trembling. "My grandmother has also said that men desire me because of my beauty, and they might take me to wife, whether I want them or not. I do not want to be a wife or a concubine, Reverend Father. It is my wish to remain a virgin until I die."

The priest nodded. "Thank you for answering my question, my daughter. Now I will answer your question. All nuns must make a vow of virginity. Maidens who are not nuns may also make such vows, but they may find them harder to keep."

"How would I make such a vow?"

"It is much the same as when a vassal swears fealty to the king. Surely you have seen such?" The maiden nodded. The priest continued. "When you have fasted and confessed your sins and been shriven, you kneel before God, acknowledge him as your lord, and promise him your virginity."

"Thank you, Reverend Father."

"May God keep you, child," he replied. He watched her walk down the aisle to the door of the church. She turned and signed herself with the cross, then left. Her maidservant followed behind her.

Over the next fortnight, Lord Radobertus spent more time with King Dagobert, listening to the petitions that local people brought, writing up the king's judgments, reviewing documents and sealing them with the king's ring, and sending messages by courier to various nobles throughout the kingdom. Many of the messages went to Lord Siwinus, the sworn friend of Lord Radobertus, who would be next to host the king and his company and who, at the Mass for the Feast of the Exaltation of the Cross, would be made a referendary to the king. In a separate correspondence with Lord Radobertus, Lord Siwinus had also agreed that his son, Ansbert, would marry Lord Radobertus's daughter in the spring, after the feast of the Resurrection.

The next week went by in a blur of hunting and hawking, drinking and dancing, while the servants packed and prepared for the journey to Lord Siwinus's lands. The day before they were to depart, Angadrisma told Berevera that she was going to the chapel to make her confession and pray.

The morning was cool and gray, with a fine mist in the air. The trees in the forest surrounding the manor were touched with orange and gold. At the door of the chapel, Angadrisma turned to Berevera. "Wait here on the porch," she said, then she slipped inside. The shutters were closed, and the chapel was dark except for the single lamp above the altar.

The priest was waiting for her. "Have you

fasted?" he asked.

"I have, Reverend Father."

"Then kneel here, before the altar, and make your confession."

Angadrisma knelt on the wooden floor. "O my God, I am heartily sorry for having offended You. I detest all my sins because of your just punishments, but most of all because they offend You, my God, for you are good and deserving of my love and my obedience."

The priest questioned her, listened to her, advised her, and finally absolved her of all her guilt. "Now, my child, before you arise, make your vow to the Lord."

Angadrisma placed the palms of her hands together in front of her chest, then stretched them toward the altar.

"Behold, I am a handmaiden of the Lord. I consecrate myself to You, O Christ, my Lord and my God. I promise on my honor that I will be faithful to You, and that I will live in virginity all the days of my life, by Your mercy, and with the help of Your all holy and ever virgin Mother. Amen."

On the morning that the king was to set out for Lord Siwinus's manor, Lord Egric presented gifts to the king and his retainers. Plates and goblets made of silver and gold, adorned with garnets. Garnet and gold brooches and pendants and rings. Necklaces with beads of glass and gold. Garments of silk.

Angadrisma was silently hoping the leavetaking would soon be over when Lord Egric invited her to come to him. She froze. Berevera gave her a little shove, and Angadrisma came to herself. She held herself as tall as she could, walked to where Lord Egric stood, and knelt and kissed his hand.

"Because of my love for your father, Angadrisma, and because of your beauty, I have a gift for you." A stablehand appeared as if from nowhere. He was leading the black mare. "This horse captured your heart when you arrived at my estate. It is now yours."

Angadrisma knelt and kissed Lord Egric's hand again. "Thank you, my lord," she said.

Then it was time to leave.

"Grandmama, may I ride today?" Angadrisma asked.

"Yes, Angadrisma," Dame Wulfgurd replied. "You will no longer walk with the children when we travel. You will ride next to me, and Berevera will walk alongside you."

"Oh, Grandmama, thank you!" said Angadrisma, with a smile as bright as the sun.

Although the road between Lord Egric's land and that of Lord Siwinus was narrow and rough, the weather was dry, and they made good time, arriving before the sixth hour at the clearing where dinner would be served. Trees that had been cut to make the clearing had been transformed into benches and tables. The king's throne was set up on a small platform, with benches next to him for the principal court officials. When everyone was seated according to their rank and the blessing had been said, the servants brought out the food. At the king's table, there was a shoulder of pork surrounded by stews of various kinds. For the rest, men and women alike, there were platters of cold bacon, loaves of white bread, crocks of butter, a dozen different kinds of cheese, and well-cooked turnips dipped in honey and pork fat, along with pitchers of perry and beer.

When the meal was done and the horses

and mules had been watered and rested, they resumed their journey. The road was wider here, and the young noblemen raced their horses through the procession, jumping and turning as if on a battlefield. The older noblemen laughed and shouted and placed bets on the men and horses. When the races were over and the bets settled, the men sang to pass the time, starting with ribald songs of lust and lechery, and then songs of home and hearth. The sun had set before they reached the camp, and fires were burning to welcome them.

They arrived at Lord Siwinus's castle late on the third day. The drawbridge across the dry moat was already down, and Lord Siwinus himself stood at the gate to welcome the king.

After Mass the next morning, Angadrisma watched the other children run off to explore Lord Siwinus's estate. She walked from the chapel, past the stables, and back to the hall. Dame Wulfgurd was sitting on a chest in the parlor, spinning linen thread as fine as a spider web.

"Grandmama," she said to Dame Wulfgurd, "would you go with me to the stable? I would like to see that Bella is being properly cared for."

Dame Wulfgurd looked to Lord Radobertus. "My son, would you permit Angadrisma to go to the stable if I am with her?"

Lord Radobertus looked at his daughter, who looked back at him imploringly. "Yes, Mama," he said. "She is responsible for her mare, so if you are with her, she may go."

Dame Wulfgurd stood and set her spindle and distaff on the chest. "Let us go," she said.

"When you return," said Lord Radobertus, "I will have some news for you, Angadrisma."

"Is it good news?" asked Angadrisma.

"It is very good news, my child," said Lord Radobertus with a smile. "Now give me a kiss, and then go." Angadrisma knelt and kissed his hand, then rose and kissed his cheek.

The stable was an impressive structure. The lower part of the walls were stone. Above the stone, there were large windows that would let in light and air. Somewhere inside, a man was singing. Dame Wulfgurd stopped just outside the stable door. "It is your mare, my child. I will watch and listen. You must see to her care."

Angadrisma nodded and stepped through the stable doors. "Is the count of the stable here?" she said in a voice loud enough for anyone in the building to hear.

The singing stopped. A man stepped out of one of the stalls. "I am Bertric, count of the stable, Madam," he said.

"I would see that my mare is being cared for properly," said Angadrisma.

"Yours is the black mare?" Count Bertric asked.

"Yes. She was called Death before, but now she is mine, and I call her Bella."

"Some of the grooms are afraid of Bella, so I have taken charge of her myself," said Count Bertric. "She is in the second stall from the end. I've put other mares in the stalls on either side of her, so they can get to know each other before I put them out in the pasture together."

Angadrisma nodded. "That is wise," she said. Bella heard her voice and whickered.

Count Bertric opened the stall door. Angadrisma went in and patted Bella on the withers, then stroked the side of her face. "You like that, don't you, Bella?" she said. "Papa's horse would bite my hand if I tried to stroke his face." She checked that the water in Bella's bucket was clear, the bedding was clean, and the hayrack was full, then she examined Bella's hooves.

"Do you wish to inspect her tack?" Count Bertric asked.

"Thank you," said Angadrisma, "but my father will be waiting for us. I will check on Bella again tomorrow and inspect the tack then."

"Yes, Madam," said Count Bertric.

Angadrisma patted Bella once more, then left the stall. "Thank you, Count Bertric," she said.

"I am ever at your service, Madam," he replied.

Lord Radobertus was waiting when Angadrisma and Dame Wulfgurd entered the parlor. Angadrisma knelt and kissed her father's hand, then stood and kissed his cheek. "Do you have news for me, Papa?" she asked.

"I do," he said. "When Lord Siwinus and I met today, we signed the marriage contract." He smiled broadly. "You and Ansbert will be wed after Pentecost."

"Papa, what? I – no, I cannot marry Ansbert. Not now."

"Oh, child, of course you can't marry him now. By Pentecost, though, you will both be of age, and then you shall marry."

"But Papa! Papa, I can't. I don't want to be a wife or a concubine."

"A concubine? Angadrisma, where do you get such ideas? You will not be a concubine, nor will Ansbert take a concubine. Lord Siwinus is a pious man, and he is raising his son in faith and piety. Ansbert will have no other wife than you, and you alone."

Angadrisma's mind swirled with a thousand thoughts, but no words would come.

"Radobertus," said Dame Wulfgurd, "this is too much for her to take in all at once. Look how pale she is. Berevera, go get a flagon of hot spiced wine. Be quick. Here, Angadrisma, sit on this stool."

Angadrisma let herself be guided to the stool. She sat without speaking. Dame Wulfgurd put a fur around her shoulders, then looked at Lord Radobertus. "She is a young maiden,

Radobertus. She has no memory of her mother, no idea of the blessing of a pious and faithful marriage."

"I am afraid," said Angadrisma.

"Of course you are, my child," said Dame Wulfgurd. "You are young and beautiful, and you are surrounded by wolves. When you are married to Ansbert, when you are the wife of the son of one of the king's referendaries, you shall have nothing more to fear."

"I thought she would rejoice to hear this news," said Lord Radobertus softly.

"You have never been a young maiden, my son," said Dame Wulfgurd.

Berevera came in carrying a basket with a flagon of wine and three goblets. Lord Radobertus's manservant took the basket from her, filled a goblet, and handed it to Lord Radobertus. Lord Radobertus gave it to Angadrisma. "Drink, my child," he said.

Angadrisma drank but said nothing.

"My lord, the bell has rung for dinner," said Berevera.

"We must go," said Lord Radobertus.

"We will send a serving maid with spiced wine," said Dame Wulfgurd.

When only Berevera remained in the parlor, Angadrisma looked up. "I would be alone," she said.

"Yes, Madam," she replied. "I will be on the other side of the drapes, if you should need anything."

"I need nothing," Angadrisma replied.

Angadrisma closed her eyes and saw herself in the chapel at Lord Egric's manor, making her vow of virginity. She slipped off the stool and onto the stone floor of the chamber, where she knelt to pray. "O Christ Jesus, I am filled with confusion. I consecrated myself to you as my Lord, and I want none other than you." Tears began to flow down Angadrisma's face. She wiped them away with the back of her hand. "Christ my God, I don't know how to defy my father, but I know I must not break my vow to you. If my beauty has caused men to want me, then take my beauty away from me and grant me some other blessing, some other gift, that would cause men to turn away from me. By your grace and mercy, with the help of your Holy and Virgin

Mother, help me, O God."

As she remained on her knees, a feeling of warmth came over her. Her breathing slowed. The tears stopped flowing. She felt at peace. She took a deep breath, then wiped her face with her hands once more. It hurt. Her face and her hands hurt. She looked at her hands. They were covered with open sores. She touched her face, gently. It was covered with sores as well.

"Thanks be to God!" she breathed. "Oh, thank you, my Lord Jesus. Thank you." She pushed herself up off the floor. "Berevera!" she said. "I need you."

Berevera was in the parlor in an instant. She placed the flagon of wine on the table, then turned to Angadrisma. She looked at her, then closed her eyes and shook her head. She looked again. "Angadrisma," she said slowly, "your face is covered in sores."

"And my hands," Angadrisma replied, holding them up for Berevera to see. "I think they may cover my whole body."

"God help us!" said Berevera. "Stay here. I will summon your father and Brother Adalmund."

Brother Adalmund, the court physician, inspected the sores on Angadrisma's hands and face, felt her pulse, and evaluated her urine. When he was done with his examination, he spoke to her softly. "Madam, God has granted you the gift of leprosy. If you accept it patiently, when you die, you will not suffer the pains of Purgatory, but will be escorted by the angels directly to God's presence in Heaven."

Dame Wulfgurd stiffened. "Are you quite certain this is leprosy?" she asked. "Her skin was entirely unblemished yesterday. I have never heard of leprosy advancing so rapidly. Have you considered the evil eye?"

"I have considered it, Madam," replied Brother Adalmund. "While it is true that her condition has advanced rapidly, I do not see the signs of the evil eye. It is simply leprosy, which progresses at different rates in different people, according to the will of God."

"Is there nothing you can do?" asked Lord Radobertus.

"There is much that can be done to ensure her comfort and well-being," replied Adalmund.

"What of a cure?" asked Lord Radobertus.

"Papa, Papa, I desire no cure," said

Angadrisma. "This affliction is a gift from God."

"She must have a quiet space," said Brother Adalmund. "We will set screens in the corner over here, where she can rest. She must have clean food, pure water, sweet music, and healthful air. I will bring ointments and teach Berevera how to anoint the sores, and I will bring a draught to help her sleep. Although she should sleep alone, she must have companions who visit her and activities that cheer her. In the spring, she may make a pilgrimage to the shrine of St. Evrou at St. Peter's Abbey, for many there find healing."

"I will speak to Lord Siwinus and the king," said Lord Radobertus.

The lords Radobertus and Siwinus sat on the stone bench beneath the oak tree. "My heart overflows with sorrow, Siwinus, my friend, and my mind is filled with darkness and confusion. I cannot think. Tell me, what options do we have for Angadrisma?"

"She cannot travel with the king. She needs more care than seems possible for a member of his entourage. When the king leaves, she must stay behind."

"I would rather she reside at my castle than a lazar house," said Lord Radobertus.

"I would rather she reside here," said Lord Siwinus. "It will be her home after she marries Ansbert."

"What? No! No, my friend, she cannot marry Ansbert. The wedding contract must be annulled."

"I sealed that contract with a solemn oath, and I would not break it."

"I also swore an oath," said Lord Radobertus, "and yet out of love for you, I would have the contract annulled." Lord Siwinus started to speak, and Lord Radobertus held up his hand. "You swore that Ansbert would have neither wife nor concubine, save Angadrisma alone. Yet Angadrisma's affliction means that the marriage would be unconsummated. That is too much to ask of Ansbert."

Lord Siwinus scowled. "I would not ask," he said. "I would command."

"No, my friend. We must send for Archbishop Ouen to absolve us of the oaths we swore and annul the contract."

Angadrisma sat on a stool in the parlor, looking at the horses that raced across the curtains and up the walls, wondering whether Brother Adalmund would allow her to ride. When her father and Lord Siwinus entered, she knelt before her father and bowed her head over his hand, then stood.

"Lord Siwinus and I would talk with you, my child," said Lord Radobertus.

"Yes, Papa."

Lord Radobertus sat on the edge of Lord Siwinus's bed, and Lord Siwinus pulled a bench over so that he could sit beside Angadrisma.

Lord Radobertus began. "Angadrisma, your affliction will make it difficult for you to travel with the king, yet I would not wish you to live among strangers in a lazar house."

"Your father and I have signed a marriage contract," said Lord Siwinus, "and I will honor the contract. You and Ansbert will marry, and you will live here. We can provide you with everything you need for your comfort and, if God wills it, for your healing."

"No, Lord Siwinus. No! I am no longer a suitable wife for Ansbert. You and my father must annul the marriage contract, and you must make another match for Ansbert."

Lord Siwinus took Angadrisma's hands in his and looked into her eyes. "If it is it truly your will," he said, "we will ask Archishop Ouen to release us from the vows that we made when we signed the contract. If instead you desire to marry Ansbert, you will marry him."

"It is my will to end the marriage contract," she said firmly. "I vowed my virginity to Christ before I knew of the plans you and my father had for me. Our Lord Christ has protected my vow by sending me leprosy."

The lords Radobertus and Siwinus looked at each other for what seemed like an eternity. Finally Lord Radobertus spoke. "When did you make this vow, my child?"

"I made it the day before we left Lord Egric's manor," she replied.

"Are there witnesses to the vow?" asked Lord Siwinus.

"Yes. The priest blessed me to take the vow, and he witnessed it."

"Why did you not tell me of the vow, Angadrisma?" asked Lord Radobertus.

"I don't know, Papa. You were so busy, and

I never thought that you would make a marriage contract for me without telling me. Then, when you told me you had made the contract, I didn't know how to tell you. I was afraid you would force me to give up my vow." Angadrisma paused. "I was wrong not to tell you. Please forgive me."

"Blessed daughter, of course I forgive you." His voice was choked. "You must forgive me as well."

"Oh, Papa, what have I to forgive?"

Lord Radobertus shook his head and looked to Lord Siwinus.

"Before you were born, Angadrisma," Lord Siwinus said, "a council of the church decreed that a woman or a girl who was consecrated to God could not be forced to give up the consecrated life, not even by royal decree. By making the marriage contract after you took your vow, your father and I have sinned against God, and against you." He knelt before her. "Forgive me."

Angadrisma looked from him to her father and back again. "I forgive," she said, "and God forgives."

Lord Siwinus rose. "We have work to do,

Radobertus. Since she has vowed a consecrated life, we must find a convent that will accept her."

"When we ask Archbishop Ouen to absolve us of the vows," Lord Radobertus said, "we will ask him to find a place for her."

Lord Radobertus found Lord Siwinus inspecting the apiary. "I have news from the archbishop," he said.

"So soon? It has been but a week."

"It seems our archbishop appreciated the urgency of our request."

"What does he say?" asked Lord Siwinus.

"I haven't read it yet. I thought we should read it together."

"Thank you, my friend," said Lord Siwinus.

Lord Radobertus took a small wooden box from under his cloak. "Hold this," he said. "The courier said to treat it with reverence and care."

Lord Siwinus took the box with both hands. Lord Radobertus brought out the letter, broke the seal, and began to read. "Ouen, by the grace of God archbishop of Rouen, to his venerable and beloved friend Radobertus, referendary and ringbearer to the god-protected King Dagobert, the first of that name, his pastoral blessing and most kind greeting. My dear son, it was with great sorrow that I read of your daughter's affliction. Out of paternal affection for you and Lord Siwinus, and pastoral care for your Angadrisma and Ansbert, I declare that the affliction that has come upon Angadrisma is an impediment to marriage. I therefore absolve you and Lord Siwinus of all oaths, vows, and promises made regarding the marriage of Angadrisma and Ansbert and hereby annul the marriage contract.

"Yet, while Angadrisma will not marry Ansbert, I greatly regret that I cannot create a place for her at a convent. Although I have the keys to heaven, the abbesses hold the keys to their houses. I cannot command an abbess to accept a leper into her community. Assure Angadrisma of my fervent prayers on her behalf and ask her to accept the reliquary that is conveyed with this letter as a gift for her salvation. The reliquary contains a relic of Saint Evrou. Give my warmest greetings to your venerable and pious mother and to the honorable Lord Siwinus. May Almighty God grant you mercy and keep you and all yours in his tender care."

Lord Siwinus stared at the box in his hands. "A priceless gift," he said. "What did you offer as a dowry for the convent that would take Angadrisma?"

"The same as I had offered you," said Lord Radobertus.

"That is a handsome offer," said Lord Siwinus. "Yet the first offer doesn't have to be the last. She would bring with her this relic. What if I were to provide a chapel to house it? And what if the king were to provide an endowment?"

"Lord Siwinus, yes. Let us go to the king."

Many more letters went between Lord Radobertus and Archbishop Ouen. At last it was settled. On the first day of Advent, at the convent called the Oratory, Archbishop Ouen would bestow the veil on Angadrisma, and she would become a sister of that house.

Dame Wulfgurd took charge of planning the journey to Beauvais. It would take four days, if the weather was good. This time of year, though, the weather would not be good. She planned for eight days and hoped for six. She and Lord Radobertus would go, of course. Lord

Siwinus insisted on being part of the retinue. Count Bertric would attend the horses. Berevera, other servants, and a small company of mounted warriors would travel with them.

"I will ride Bella to Beauvais," Angadrisma said.

Dame Wulfgurd shook her head. "You will not," she said. "Your visage may frighten people when we ride by, and people who are frightened are dangerous."

"I will wear a veil."

Dame Wulfgurd shook her head. "It is against my judgment, but I will permit it. You will ride between me and your father."

When they arrived at the convent, the porter called for grooms to attend the horses and for Sister Madelgarde to attend the guests.

"I will go with the horses," said Count Bertric firmly.

"Our grooms will care for your horses," replied the porter, just as firmly. "You will remain here with the other guests until Sister Madelgarde gives you leave to go to the stables."

"Your grooms may fear the black mare,"

Count Bertric said.

"Our grooms have no fear of pagan superstitions," replied the porter.

As servants unloaded the carts and grooms took the horses, Sister Madelgarde arrived. She sent messages to the kitchen and provided instructions to all the guests except Angadrisma, who stood with her hand on the black mare's withers. A tiny nun with a weathered face approached Angadrisma. "I am Sister Ingoberg," she said. "I have charge of novices. You no longer have need of your luggage or your horse or your servant. Leave them here. Follow me."

Angadrisma followed Sister Ingoberg across the courtyard, through a gate, and down a long corridor to a small room. The room was furnished with a bench and a brazier. A white linen tunic was neatly folded on the bench.

"You may remove your veil," said Sister Ingoberg.

Angadrisma hesitated.

"Every woman here has served at the lazar house at one time or another, my child. Your appearance will not cause fear or distress."

Angadrisma removed the veil.

Sister Ingoberg studied her face. "Are you in pain?"

"No, Sister. God, in His mercy, gave me leprosy, but He has spared me any pain."

"Thanks be to God. Now, remove your garments and your jewels, and dress yourself in the tunic."

Angadrisma removed her mantle and her silk tunic and laid them across the bench. She winced as she pulled off her underdress, which was stuck to her sores. "Would you have me wear another underdress between my skin and the tunic?" she asked Sister Ingoberg.

"There is no need," Sister Ingoberg replied. Angadrisma pulled the white linen tunic over her head. "Now you will follow me to the chapel," said Sister Ingoberg. "Archbishop Ouen is waiting for you."

"I feel naked," said Angadrisma.

"Indeed," said Sister Ingoberg.

There were but a few steps from the changing room to a narrow door that opened into the chapel nave. Angadrisma signed herself with the cross as they entered.

"Go stand before the steps to the altar,"

Sister Ingoberg said.

Angadrisma did as she was instructed. Archbishop Ouen approached her. They spoke quietly. She knelt, made her confession, and received absolution. The archbishop told her to stand. She stood.

"My daughter, you will spend this night here. You will prayerfully consider the vows you have made and the vows you will make on the morrow. When I return, I will ask you if you intend to proceed. If you do not, I will free you from all vows that you have made, and you will depart this convent with your family. Do you understand?"

"Yes, my lord," Angadrisma replied.

"If, on the morrow, you still wish to become a nun, you will receive the veil from me. Sister Ingoberg will dress you in the monastic habit, and I will place on your hand the ring that marks you as a bride of Christ. Have you any questions?"

"No, my lord."

"Kneel here, then, my daughter. No one will disturb you until I return to you."

Angadrisma knelt on the stone floor, and

Archbishop Ouen and Sister Ingoberg left the chapel.

Shortly before the first hour of the morning, Archbishop Ouen and Sister Ingoberg returned. Sister Ingoberg stood by the door. Archbishop Ouen walked across the chapel and stood beside Angadrisma. "Stand, my daughter," he said.

Angadrisma tried to stand and found that her legs were too stiff to move. "Forgive me, reverend lord, but I need your help to rise."

Archbishop Ouen blessed her with the sign of the cross, then put his hand under her elbow and lifted her to her feet. She wobbled a bit, then found her balance and stood.

"Have you considered your decision?" he asked her.

"I have, reverend lord."

"Tell me, then, is it your will to stay here, or to leave?"

"Reverend lord, I will have no other husband than Christ. It is my will to stay."

He nodded to Sister Ingoberg, who left. Then, turning to Angadrisma, he said, "Sister

Ingoberg will have the mistress of guests bring your family here to witness your vows. She will also bring a small choir of nuns to take part in the service. When the service is over, you will bid farewell to your family, and Sister Ingoberg will take you to the dormitory. You will learn from her all you need to know to be a sister of this house. Have you any questions?"

"No, reverend lord."

"Then kneel here, and wait."

Angadrisma knelt and waited. She heard the sounds of people entering the chapel, the hushed voice of her father, the almost-silent steps of the nuns. Her face felt as though she stood in the sunlight on a summer day, and a breath of air moved about her. Archbishop Ouen invoked God's blessing on the service about to begin, and the nuns began chanting, their voices echoing so that it sounded like all of the nuns on earth and in heaven were part of the song.

Archbishop Ouen prayed God's blessings on the convent and the king, on the planting and the harvest, on travelers, the sick, and those in prison. The nuns chanted the response to each blessing. Finally, he prayed God's blessing on Angadrisma herself. The warmth in her face spread throughout her body, and the breath of air grew faintly stronger. A wisp of her uncovered hair moved onto her face. She resisted the urge to move it away.

After another lengthy prayer, Archbishop Ouen blessed the veil and placed it on her head, saying "Receive, O virgin of Christ, the veil of virginity." As the veil touched her head, the breath of air became a gentle breeze, fluttering the end of the veil. The warmth became more intense. She felt as though she had stepped into a fire that burned but did not consume.

"Arise, daughter," said Archbishop Ouen. Angadrisma stood. She looked at the archbishop, and he looked at her, for what seemed like a very long time. He turned and picked up his blessing cross from the altar and blessed her with it. "Kiss the cross, Angadrisma," he said softly. She kissed it. He looked at her longer.

"Turn and face the people," he said. She turned. "Rejoice, O virgin of Christ, for God has made you whole." Angadrisma remained silent. "Angadrisma, my daughter," he said, "rejoice. Your bridegroom, Christ our God, has given you a nuptial gift. God has removed your affliction. Your faith has made you whole."

He looked out over the people. "Lord Radobertus, rejoice! Your daughter is no longer afflicted with leprosy. Dame Wulfgurd, rejoice, for she is healed! All of you, look at what God has done, and rejoice!"

As Angadrisma stood wondering at his words, the choir began to sing an alleluia that was not part of the service. Sister Ingobert brought the raiment of a nun and held it out to Archbishop Ouen. He blessed it. When the choir completed the alleluia, she dressed Angadrisma there, before the people. Then Archbishop Ouen blessed the ring, took Angadrisma's right hand, and placed the ring on her third finger. "Receive, O blessed virgin of Christ, your eternal Bridegroom."

The choir resumed chanting the service, which was soon completed.

"Now go to your father and your grandmother," said Sister Ingobert. "Give them the honor that is their due, then return to me."

Angadrisma walked serenely to Dame Wulfgurd. She knelt, and Dame Wulfgurd stroked her face in wonder. Angadrisma kissed her hand, then rose and kissed her cheek. She stood there a moment, then walked across the chapel to where her father and Lord Siwinus stood. She knelt before her father, kissed his hand, then rose and kissed his cheek. Turning to

Lord Siwinus, she said, "You were almost my father, and if you will accept it, I will give you a filial kiss." He nodded. She knelt, kissed his hand, then rose and kissed his cheek.

"I must go now," she said. "May you all fare as well as I fare, by God's mercy."

"By God's mercy," said Dame Wulfgurd. "Amen."

St. Angadrisma

Some stories say that Ansbert, the son of Siwinus, had also taken a vow of virginity, but most sources agree that he took a wife after the marriage contract with Angadrisma was annulled. He became a referendary of Chlothar III, the son of Clovis II and grandson of Dagobert I. Later, he became a monk, then an abbot, and in 683, he succeeded Ouen as Archibishop of Rouen.

As for Angadrisma, she became the abbess of the Oroër-des-Vierges (in English, the Oratory of the Virgins), the convent which had accepted her as a leper. She lived for many long years and died in peace in the year 695. Ansbert and Radobertus also died that same year. The convent was destroyed by the Normans in 851.

Prayer
Saint Angadrisma of the Oratory, because you chose to serve Christ without ceasing, he gave you the grace to work miracles. Pray to God that He grant to our souls great mercy!

St. John the Little
Born 339, Thebes, Egypt
Died 409, Mountain of St. Anthony, Egypt

FEAST DAY NOVEMBER 9

For the first time since their parents had died, Daniel and John were hungry. The remains from the funeral meal had sustained them over the first days of their grief. Now the food was gone. They had no money and no patron and no idea how they were going to provide for themselves, so they sat in the shade of the acacia tree, and they argued.

"If we were monks at Scetis, we would not have to work. We would spend our days in prayer," said John. "Not just morning and night, but always."

"Listen to me, John. We need to eat," said Daniel. "The Holy Apostle Paul said that if a man does not work, he should not eat."

"What of the monks, then? They eat, and they do not work."

"We are not monks, John. We are ordinary men. We are like our First Father, Adam. God told him to work in the garden. Like our First Father, and like our own father, we must work. If you're going to spend your days praying, pray that we find work."

John looked up at the leaves over their heads, and the shards of blue between the leaves. "Are we not called to lay aside all earthly cares?" he asked. "Look at the sky, Daniel. See the heavens spread out above us? Are we not supposed to put our minds on the things of heaven? Did not our Lord God himself command us to live like the birds of the air and the lilies of the field? They do not work, but the Lord provides for them."

Daniel shook his head. "John," he said. "John, my brother, lay aside this nonsense, and let us talk about how we shall find work."

"I will be like the angels, Daniel. It will be my work to ceaselessly offer praise to God." With that, John leapt to his feet, threw off his cloak, and ran. Daniel stayed under the tree and watched him go.

The weather changed over the next few days. The days became cooler, the nights cold for someone without a cloak. Daniel walked up the crumbling stairs to the roof of their house every evening and every morning to watch for his brother, as the father of the Prodigal had watched for his son.

One evening, Daniel walked wearily down the stairs and went inside. The single room was dark. Where there should have been lamps to light at the setting of the sun, there were only empty niches in the wall. There were no shelves, no baskets, no cooking pots, no sickles or winnowing forks, nothing of any value. Daniel had sold it all to pay for their parents' funeral. He kept only the water jars, a wooden drinking vessel, the chamber pots, and the sleeping rugs. He barred the door, said his prayers, shook out his sleeping rug, and laid down on the floor. He was somewhere between sleeping and waking when a small sound disturbed him. A rat? No, not a rat. There was a person at the door.

"Who is there?" Daniel called out.

"Daniel! It is me! John! Your brother! I have come back. Let me in!"

Daniel was overcome with joy and relief. He sat up, then stopped. "My brother has become an angel," he said. "He no longer lives among men."

"Daniel! I'm hungry and cold. Let me in, Daniel. Let me in!" So it went, for minutes or hours. John finally gave up and sat on the ground. He wrapped his arms around his knees and leaned against the door. Daniel laid himself back down on his sleeping rug. They both shed silent tears as they fell asleep.

Before it was light, when the first roosters crowed, Daniel got up from the floor, washed his face and hands, said his prayers, and opened the door. John looked up at him. "Come in, my brother," Daniel said. "You are a man. You must work in order to eat." John stood up, then made a prostration, the first time (but not the last) that he prostrated himself before his brother, and he said, simply, "Forgive me."

Daniel gave his forgiveness. He found labor for them here and there. Some days, they hauled melons from the port to the market for a shopkeeper, or washed laundry at the riverbank, keeping an eye out for crocodiles as they worked. Some days, they made mud for a craftsman who repaired the walls of the houses of the wealthy. If Daniel could find them no other work, they joined a city crew cleaning night waste from the streets. Daniel didn't like working for the city crews, because they didn't sing as they worked.

Yet the city paid them in coin, while the shopkeepers in kind. The craftsman who repaired walls had known their parents. He also paid them in coin, and he added to their wages a day's ration of bread and beer. When they had gone too many days without food, they would visit the almoner at the cathedral, who would give them each a loaf of flat bread with his blessing.

They took the bread home, asked God's blessing on the bread, and sat in the shade of the acacia tree to eat.

"Is this not a meal suitable for a monk, my brother?" asked John.

"A loaf of plain flat bread," said Daniel. He took a bite, chewed and swallowed. "Yes, John, this is a meal for a monk, or for a poor man. Men like us."

"You see, my brother? Poor men, men like us, live in asceticism. We eat like monks. Our hunger wakes us during the night, and we pray like monks. We must go to Scetis and become monks."

Daniel sighed. "John, my brother, I love you. I am tired and hungry, and I do not want to talk about going to Scetis. Our life is here."

"Your life, you mean. If you will not go with me, I will go alone."

"John! No, John, you must not go alone. What if something happened to you? John, I love you. You are all I have. You must not go."

"I will go, and I will not come back."

The brothers stared at each other. Finally, Daniel looked away. He took a deep breath, then looked back at his brother. "You speak the truth, John. You are a dwarf. You will not come back because some rich man's servants will capture you and put you in their master's menagerie, and you will live in a cage with the wild beasts, and they will bring you out at feasts to amuse their guests."

"Daniel, no. No, that could not happen."

"It could, my brother. You know it could. If it does not happen, you could drown in the river, or be eaten by a crocodile, or wander the desert looking for the hidden monasteries until you died of hunger or thirst or became the prey of lions. If you went alone, I would not be there to protect you."

"Then go with me," John pleaded.

"How can we go?" Daniel said. "We have nothing. Our parents are dead. We have no patron. We earn barely enough to eat. It takes money to travel, John, and we have no money.

We have nothing. Nothing! How will we make our way to the monastery?"

"You are right, my brother. We have nothing in Thebes. If we go, we will have nothing for the journey. That changes nothing. We are nothing. So I shall go and be nothing in the desert, hidden from the world that has never seen me anyway. Go with me, Daniel, and be nothing with me."

Then rent came due. Daniel had known, of course, that his father paid rent every year for their home. Grief and fear and hunger and hard labor had driven the thought from his mind. The rent was not much, but it was infinitely more than nothing. What was there to do besides go to Scetis? Perhaps they would die together on the way. They might as well die seeking God in the desert as seeking work in Thebes.

They closed the door of their home behind them, taking only the clothes they wore and a sleeping rug for each of them. When they told the almoner at the cathedral where they were going, he gave them each an extra loaf of bread and arranged passage for them on a small boat going down the Nile.

It was the first month of the inundation. The air was hot, the water was running high, and the journey was swift. The mariners managed the sails with skill and songs. When they reached the port nearest the valley where they would find the monasteries, the captain gave them each a waterskin and a loaf of bread and pointed them to the road that would take them to Scetis.

The journey on foot seemed endless, the dangers greater than Daniel had ever imagined. Finally, after they knew not how many nights had passed, they found themselves standing at the edge of the desolate valley that hid Scetis from the world.

Heat shimmered in the air ahead of them. "The sun is high, my brother. We have gone far enough today," said Daniel. "We will find shade here, then go down into the valley when evening comes."

"Which of those patches of green do you think is the monastery?" asked John.

"How would I know?" asked Daniel. He walked back the way they had come, looking for a spot that would shelter them from the sun. He found a small outcrop of rocks that would have to suffice. "John," he called out. "John, come here!" There was no answer. He turned to look at where he had left John standing. John was nowhere in sight.

"My brother," Daniel said under his breath. He walked back to the valley's edge. His brother was running down the road as if he had wings on his feet.

John had collapsed onto the ground and was still panting hard when Daniel caught up with him. "We are almost there!" John said between gasps.

"How would you know?" said Daniel.

"Look, Daniel! Do you not see the dwelling places of the hermits?"

Daniel looked across the valley. Here and there were mounds that could be huts. They could equally well be boulders.

When John could breathe again, he sat up. A small lizard, the color of the sand, scampered up the rock next to him, then ran back down the other side and disappeared.

"Let's go there," John said, pointing to one of the huts, if a hut it was.

"Lead the way," said Daniel. "If it's a boulder, we can shelter against it until night."

It was indeed a hut, made of mud and straw like so many of the houses in Thebes. Before John could knock, the door opened, and an old man with a long silver beard looked out at them. His skin was dark and leathery, and he was wearing a cloak and cowl, with a staff in his hand.

"I have been expecting you," he said. "Follow me."

They walked behind the old man in the silence of midday. The air smelled of dust and heat.

At last they approached a small stone building. The door opened, and an old man with a dark beard stepped out of the building and into the light.

John and Daniel prostrated themselves before the old man.

"Welcome John and Daniel," he said. "I am Ammoes. God has granted me charge over this monastery. With wisdom, with the fear of God, stand and tell me why you are here."

John and Daniel stood. "Reverend Father," said John. "If God has told you my name, you know why I am here. I want to be a monk, and to live like the angels. If you ask God, he will give me to you, so that you can teach me everything concerning holiness."

Abba Ammoes turned to Daniel. "What of you?" he said.

"In truth, reverend Father, I came here out of love for my brother. God took our parents and left John to me, and when his heart was set to come here, I could not let him go alone. If you allow him to stay here, I will stay. If you send him away, I will leave with him and go wherever God directs us."

Abba Ammoes nodded, then turned back to John. "You are small and weak, my son, and the desert is harsh. Here, we must work in order to eat."

John opened his mouth, as if to speak, then stopped. Abba Ammoes turned and walked away. Daniel and John looked at each other. "Do not be afraid," said the hermit who had brought them to Abba Ammoes. "Follow me. I will take you to our guest master. He will provide you food and shelter until God shows Abba Ammoes His plans for you."

On the third day, when the sky was growing light and the full moon was low in the western sky, the old hermit came to where Daniel and John were lodging.

"Abba Ammoes will see you now," the hermit said. John and Daniel walked behind him back to the stone building where they had met Abba Ammoes. Abba Ammoes stood in front of his door, waiting for them.

Daniel and John prostrated themselves. "Stand," said Abba Ammoes. When they were on their feet, he said, "An angel came to me last night as I prayed. He told me that God had sent you here. I will shave your head, John. You will discard the clothes you are wearing, and I will put on you the clothes of a monk."

"May it be done to me according to your word," said John, his voice barely more than a whisper.

"Once it is done, you will live with me, to learn obedience and silence. Daniel, you will go with our brother here, who has grown old and needs an attendant to serve him. He will shave your head and clothe you, and he will teach you all that God wants you to know."

Daniel bowed deeply to Abba Ammoes, then embraced his brother and kissed him on both cheeks.

"Follow me," said the old hermit. Daniel bowed to him, then followed him back to his hut.

It was shortly after the sixth hour on the second day of Lent. John was sitting on the floor of the cell he shared with Abba Ammoes, weaving a basket. At least, he was trying to weave a basket. He was supposed to say the Jesus prayer as he worked, but making the basket come out evenly took every bit of concentration that he had.

He did not notice Abba Ammoes come to the door. Abba Ammoes stood silently until, finally, John looked up. "Abba!" said John.

"Follow me," said Abba Ammoes, and he turned and walked away, chanting psalms as he walked. John jumped up and followed him.

They walked past a small lake surrounded by dried mudflats crusted with salt. Here and there were small plants with leathery leaves. He wondered what they were, but he did not ask.

At last Abba Ammoes stopped. They had reached a circle of large stones. In the center of this circle a dry stick, about the same height as John, had been driven into the ground.

"Look at this stick," said Abba Ammoes. John looked at it in silence. "You must water this stick every day until it bears fruit."

John looked at Abba Ammoes uncertainly. "I must water the stick?" he asked.

"You must water this stick every day until it bears fruit," Abba Ammoes replied.

John stood for a time in silence. "Where will I find water?" he asked.

"If God does not provide a spring here, then you must bring the water with you."

"Yes, Abba," John said.

Abba Ammoes turned to walk back the way they had come. John stared at the stick a moment more, then turned and followed Abba Ammoes. When they got back to their cell, John picked up the water jug next to the door, filled it at the well, and walked back to the stick, reciting the Jesus prayer as he went.

He drank a few swallows of water from the jug, then poured the rest of the water on the stick. He stood looking at it for a time, waiting to see if leaves would appear. The evening breeze touched his face. The air was cooler now. The sun had gone from the sky. It was time to leave.

He hadn't gotten far when he saw the first star appear in the sky. At that moment, he realized that it was the new moon. There would be no moonlight to guide his way, and he wouldn't be able to find his way by starlight. He had to go back to the stick and wait for morning. He looked back the way he'd come. Or the way he thought he'd come. He wasn't sure. The roar of a lion drifted across the desert like distant thunder. It was answered by the weird squeals and growls of hyenas.

John's heart was pounding wildly. He slowed his breathing and began saying the Jesus prayer. As he felt his heartbeat slow, he turned and looked around. He could see the circle of rocks. The stick was there. He walked back to the stick and sat on the ground, his back against one of the stones, and looked out into the darkness.

He thought something moved, but when he turned to look, it was gone. He sat motionless, staring where the movement had been. As the moon rose over the distant cliffs, a small fox with enormous ears came out from behind one of the rocks. It sat on the ground on the other side of the stick. The two watched each other until, at last, they both slept.

When John woke to pray the night office, the moon was high in the sky. In the distance, he could see a caravan moving away from the salt works deep in the desert. The little fox was gone.

The sky was growing light when John woke again. As he stood stiffly, he realized he had no water. He said his morning prayers, then turned towards home, asking God for mercy as he walked.

The season of planting had come for the third time since John started watering the stick. The intense heat of the inundation moderated; the nights grew cool.

The fox was perched on top of the tallest rock, waiting for him. It took a bit of bread from his hand, then watched as John slowly emptied the water jar at the foot of the stick. John set the jar on the ground, then stepped back and looked at the stick. He closed his eyes, then looked again. There were buds on the stick.

Over the days and weeks of the planting season, the buds swelled, and leaves and flowers burst forth. By the beginning of the harvest season, the flowers had turned to tiny fruit. As the season passed, the fruit grew large and began to ripen.

On the Sunday after Pascha, John asked Abba Ammoes to walk with him down the path to the dry stick. They left after the Liturgy. As they walked, John chanted the psalms, which he now knew by heart, and Abba Ammoes joined his voice to John's.

Abba Ammoes smelled the fragrance of the fruit before they reached the circle of stones. When they got to the tree, Abba Ammoes looked at the fruit, then looked at John. "By what means has this dry stick put on leaves and fruit?" he asked.

"By your prayers," John answered.

"My prayers worked with your obedience and God's mercy. Now, pull up the hem of your robe, and let me fill it with fruit." John lifted the hem of his robe to make a basket, and Abba Ammoes filled it with fruit. As they walked back to the cenobium, they sang the hymns of the Resurrection.

Abba Ammoes led John to the refectory, where the brethren still waited for Abba Ammoes. After he blessed their meal, he walked around the refectory with John, placing a fruit from the tree in the hands of each monk, saying, "Take, eat the fruit of obedience." The monks kissed his hand, then took and ate. Daniel was the last to receive one of the fruits. He kissed the hand of Abba Ammoes, then made a prostration, the first time (but not the last) that he prostrated himself before his brother.

When all had partaken, Abba Ammoes said, "The fruit is sweet, as obedience is sweet." The tree was ever after called the tree of obedience.

After this time, Abba Ammoes became sick with a great sickness, and despite the best efforts of the physicians, he did not get better. John brought him soups and broths and other wholesome foods that are good for those who are ill, spooning it into Abba Ammoes's mouth when he was too weak to hold a spoon himself. When the illness caused vomiting or flux, John kept him and his cell clean and brought in fragrant herbs to drive away the bad air.

As the days turned into weeks, then months, and years, the pain and weakness made Abba Ammoes irritable and harsh. While John tended him gently by night and by day, Abba Ammoes never spoke so much as a single word of gratitude for his labors. It did not occur to John that it should be any other way.

One day early in the harvest season, when the air was cool and fresh, Abba Ammoes asked John, "How long has it been, my son, that I have been tested with this illness?"

"It was twelve years ago that you fell ill."

"Twelve years," Abba Ammoes said softly, and then was silent. John watched his chest rise and fall and wondered if he slept.

After a time, Abba Ammoes spoke again. "John, my son, when God takes me from this world, I want you to leave this house, and go make a home for yourself by the tree of obedience. That dry stick that I planted became, through the work of your hands, a holy sacrifice. The fruit of that tree is a sign that God has accepted you and all those who will be saved by you."

John knelt by Abba Ammoes's bed, tears streaming down his face. "May it be to me according to your word."

When it was clear that Abba Ammoes's death was near, the elders of the monastery came to his cell to comfort him and surround him with their prayers. Abba Ammoes motioned for them to be silent, then called John to him. As John knelt by him, he took John's hands and kissed them and blessed him. Then, calling to the elders, he said, "Receive John, for he is an angel on earth, and not a human being," and he spoke no more.

When Abba John found himself orphaned for a second time, he did as Abba Ammoes had commanded and made himself a cell by the tree of obedience. When it was done, he returned for the last time to the cell he had shared with Abba Ammoes and gathered his few belongings, then closed the door behind him.

When he returned to his cell, a tiny fox was sitting on a stone by the tree of obedience. It had been too many years; this could not be the fox he had befriended when the tree was nothing but a dry stick. The fox watched him carry his belongings into the cell. At sunset, when he got up to bar the door for the night, the fox walked into his cell. "Welcome, little one," he said. "Do you wish to stay?" The fox sat on his sleeping mat. "That seems to be assent," he said. He closed and barred the door and went into his inner room to pray. His prayers finished, he laid down on the sleeping mat in the outer room, and he and the fox slept. He rose at midnight, washed his face and hands, and went into his inner room to chant the night office. Then he lit a lamp and opened the door so the fox could leave.

After the fox left, Abba John sat on his mat in his outer room and wove baskets while he meditated on God's mercies. When daylight came, he walked back to the main part of Scetis to get water, bread, and more rushes to make more baskets,

Eventually, he accepted the service of a young monk named Peter. Peter worked in the bakery. Each morning when he finished his work there, he would take two loaves of bread, still warm, a water jug, and two bundles of rushes. Then he walked to Abba John's cell at the tree of obedience.

"Abba John," Peter said, setting the water jar just inside the door of the cell, "what are you making today?"

"Baskets," said John.

Peter looked at it curiously. "Why is it so large?"

"What do you mean?" He stopped working and looked at what he was doing. He had not noticed when it was time to finish off this basket and start the next. "I suppose it is rather large. Perhaps I will unwork it and try again."

Peter set the rushes on the pile against the back wall of the outer room, set the bread on the stool, and picked up the empty water jar.

"Wait," said Abba John. "You have news for me."

Peter stopped. Abba John never wanted news. Never.

"As you have said, Abba John, I have heard birds singing God's praises at dawn. That is all the news that I need to hear, and all I need to share."

"Yet there is other news, and it is heavy on your heart."

Peter stood by the door, motionless.

"You may speak."

"It is about Paësia," Peter said.

"Paësia?"

"She is, or was, a wealthy woman, Abba John. When her parents died, she refused to marry. Instead, she turned her house into a hostel for travelers. Merchants could stay there, of course, and pilgrims and monastics stay there at no charge. I was there many times, before I came here."

"Yes, I know of her. Whenever the monastery has needed money, beyond what we earn from our baskets and ropes, she has given us what we needed."

"She heard the Gospel, about giving to

anyone who asks, Abba John, and that's how she lived."

"Has she died, my son?"

"Oh, Abba John, no, it's worse than that. She gave away everything she had, and she ended up with debts that were more than she could pay. Wicked men have come and imprisoned her in her own home. They have made her house a brothel, Abba John, and her creditors sell her body and keep the money. They won't let her leave until she has paid the entire debt."

"And what says the law of this?" Abba John asked.

"The law says that she will by no means get out until she has paid the last cent."

Abba John's parents had always said that the law was cruel to debtors. That's why Daniel had refused to borrow money to pay for their parents' funeral and had instead sold everything they owned. Yet he had never heard what this young monk was telling him.

"How can we help her?" Abba John asked.

"A bishop or a priest or a monk can pay her debt and take responsibility for her," Peter said. "But who is the holy man who will take responsibility for a harlot?"

"She is no such thing," said Abba John. "She is not selling herself. Rather, the law has stolen her from herself. We must redeem her and return her to herself."

"How?"

"I will ask all the monks of Scetis and Kellia for whatever coins they have received for their work. When I have collected enough to pay Paësia's debt, I will get her and take her to a women's monastery."

Word of Abba John's plan spread quickly. Some of the monks said, "While she could, she gave us charity. It is therefore not charity, but justice, if we relieve her in her distress." Others said it was not right to give alms to a woman who was living a sinful life.

Abba John visited those who refused to give justice to Paësia. Some that he visited changed their minds about her. Some didn't. Yet there were enough who felt a debt to her that he soon gathered enough to pay her debts. He rolled the money in a heavy woolen cloth, so that the coins made no sound, then secured it around his waist. He decided to leave the door to his cell ajar so that the fox could come and go. He took a water skin to the well, to fill for his journey. His brother Daniel was there waiting.

"I have bread for your journey," said Daniel, handing his brother a leather bag.

Abba John nodded. "Thank you, my brother," he said. "Pray for me, that I might not fall prey to wealthy men or lions."

"Always, my brother."

Abba John filled his water skin and set out on the road towards the west. He would be at Paësia's house in a few days.

It was afternoon when he arrived at Paësia's house. He knocked at the door. An old woman answered. "I am John of Scetis," Abba John said. "I am here to see Paësia."

The woman laughed. "You've taken all her money," she said. "What more do you want?"

"I want to talk with her."

"Go away, little man. She has a debt to pay. If you're not hiring her services, you need to leave."

"Tell her that I have something that may be

of use to her," Abba John said.

The woman closed the door. Time passed slowly as Abba John stood without moving. At last the door opened. "She will see you now," the doorkeeper said.

Abba John entered. A little girl looked at Abba John curiously. "Are you a boy or a man?" she asked. "Paësia doesn't see boys."

"You can see my beard and hear my voice," Abba John said. "I am a man."

The child nodded. "Follow me," she said, and she led Abba John to Paësia's chamber.

Abba John pushed aside the curtain. Paësia was lying on a bed, wearing a sheer linen gown and strings of pearls. "I am here if you want me," she said.

Abba John entered the chamber and sat on the bed next to her. "My daughter," he said, "I have brought gold and silver to pay your debts, if you will go with me."

Paësia froze. "You have done what?" she whispered.

"I have brought gold and silver to pay your debts and free you from this bondage. If you consent, I will take you to the women's house at the monastery of Abba Macarius, where you can live in peace. Will you go with me?"

Paësia stood and looked around her. She opened a chest, pulled out a cloak, and wrapped it around herself. "Let us go," she said.

They walked together down the hallway to the atrium. The debt collector and the doorkeeper looked up in surprise. Abba John pulled the roll of cloth from around his waist and laid it on the table between them. "Unroll the cloth and you will find that Paësia's debt is paid. I am taking responsibility for her. We are leaving now."

"You will not take Paësia," the debt collector said.

"With her consent, and with the power of God, I will," said Abba John.

"Come," said Paësia. "We can fill waterskins at the well and be gone."

Paësia and Abba John took the road to the east. They walked without speaking until the shadows in front of them were long, and they continued to walk well into the moonless night. Finally, Abba John stopped. "I will not find our road in the dark. We must stop here for the night." He walked a little way off the road and found a sheltered spot. He knelt down and scooped the sand to make a pillow and a bed for Paësia. He signed it with a cross, then made a bed for himself between Paësia and the road. "Lay you down there," he said, pointing to the place he had made for Paësia. She nodded and, signing herself with the cross, she laid down and slept.

Abba John laid down and listened to the night. He may have dozed. He woke to the small sounds of creatures moving nearby, and beyond them, the sound of voices a great distance away. The voices were singing psalms and hymns. As the voices grew louder, the sky began to grow light. All at once, the sky was torn and the air was filled with such radiant light and song that Abba John could not bear it. He covered his eyes, and at that moment Paësia cried out with joy. Abba John shielded his eyes with his arm and looked towards Paësia. Her body began to shine with the light that filled the air. The light grew brighter before it left her body and joined the light and song that filled the sky. As he tried to make sense of all that he was seeing, the light faded, the sound of singing grew more distant, and the great cleft in the sky closed behind Paësia. At last it was dark again.

Abba John wondered if he had dreamed. Paësia was still on the ground just a few steps from where he lay. He crawled across the sand toward her. "Paësia, my daughter," he said softly. She did not speak. "Paësia!" he said, more loudly. There was no response. He reached out and touched her foot. "Paësia," he whispered, but he knew she was not there. He crossed himself, then crawled back to his place in the sand and waited for the morning.

At first light, before the sun was up, while the world was still without color and the air was still, Abba John stood and, facing east, he prayed. Then he walked to where Paësia lay. She was a tall woman. He didn't know how he would carry her, but he couldn't leave her holy body here, to be torn by jackals. He took a deep breath and signed her with the cross, then knelt to arrange her body on her cloak. There was no sign of death, no rigor. For modesty, he covered her body with his cloak. Then he took the edges of her cloak in his hands and began to pull. To his surprise, Paësia seemed to weigh no more than a bundle of rushes. He pulled her to the women's house at the monastery of Abba Macarius. There, he gave her holy body to the old women, who clothed her in a linen tunic and buried her with great reverence.

The old hermit looked up from his work. "Daniel, my son, go to your brother. He is waiting for you."

Daniel set the basket he was weaving on the ground and stood. "Where will I find him?" he asked.

"Go towards the monastery of Abba Macarius. You will find him beside the road. Go to him now. Do not tarry."

Daniel turned and began walking towards the road. Waves of heat rippled up from the valley floor. He considered turning aside to get water, but the hermit had told him not to tarry. He wiped the sweat from his face with his arm and kept walking.

John closed his eyes against the brightness and the pain. He heard a voice, but there was no song. The angels that came for Paësia sang. Would the angels come for him without a song?

The voice grew louder. It was calling his name. The voice took him by the shoulders and shook him. "John, my brother! John, answer me!"

John opened his eyes. The brightness had faded. The voice was between him and the sun.

He shook his head, trying to clear his thoughts.

"John, it's Daniel. I am here."

"Daniel?" John asked, his voice like that of a raven.

"Thanks be to God," said Daniel. "You live! I was afraid I was too late. Here, I can help you up. We will walk back to Scetis, and you can tell me all that has befallen you since you left to deliver Paësia from her bondage."

John shook his head. "Can't walk," he croaked. "Fell. Leg broke." He took a deep breath. "Crawled far. No water."

"Oh, John! When did you run out of water?"

John shook his head and shrugged. "Asked God to send angels."

"God sent me instead of angels, my brother. You need water, and you need to get out of the sun."

"Angels," John murmured.

"John, if I can't get you water soon, you will die. You must ride on my back, as you did when we were children. I will carry you to the hermit's cell, where we can get you water and shade, and the hermit will tend to your injury."

"How far?" asked John.

"It is not far," said Daniel. He took John's arms and put them around his neck, then stood, pulling John slowly off the ground and onto his back. "Do not die, my brother. We'll soon be there."

Abba John did not die. He stayed with Daniel and the old hermit until he could walk and stand without pain, then he returned to his cell by the tree of obedience.

Daniel had always known that the old hermit would someday die. The hermit was old when he and John had first come to Scetis, and no man lives forever. Yet Daniel had felt that the old hermit might somehow live forever, like the Beloved Apostle. Or, if not forever, then as long as the rocks and cliffs surrounded Scetis, as long as the sun rose in the sky.

The day that the old hermit couldn't stand to pray, Daniel knew. He sat on the the floor, and tears filled his eyes and flowed down his face. The hermit, his second father, took Daniel's hands in his, and kissed them, and signed them with the cross. Then he said to Daniel, "Mercy and goodness have followed me all the days of my life," and he closed his eyes and breathed no more.

Daniel sat in the cell with the old hermit as the shadows filled the hut and night fell. He sat through the night. He wept, and when he ran out of tears, he chanted psalms. When his voice failed him, and he could chant no more, he sat in darkness and silence until the sorrow filled him and he wept again.

When day came, he called for the old men, and they buried the hermit. Daniel could not go back to the cell that he and the hermit had shared. Instead, he walked to the tree of obedience and made a cell for himself near his brother John.

The merchants that bought baskets and rope from the monks brought news of the world outside Scetis. Abba John, as was his habit, sat in his cell until the merchants and their camels and news were gone.

This day, though, his brother Daniel came into his cell, and said, "Abba John, my brother, you must hear the news the merchants brought today."

Abba John did not look up from the basket he was weaving. "Does another Paësia cry out for justice?" he asked.

"No, Abba John."

Abba John continued working in silence.

"My brother, you must listen to me. It is possible that we might all die."

"It is certain that we will."

"You speak true. Yet it is not certain that we will all die as martyrs in the next week."

Abba John stopped and looked at his brother. "Speak plainly," he said.

"The merchants say that a Berber army is coming across the land toward our valley," Daniel said. "They are killing everyone they meet, cutting trees, and poisoning wells. They will be here in a week, perhaps a bit longer. Some of the brothers wish to flee with the merchants and the men from the salt works, to save their lives. Others wish to stay and earn the crown of martyrdom. The brothers are waiting for your wisdom."

Abba John set aside the reeds and basket and stood up. "God knows how little wisdom I have. Even so, I will speak."

Abba John walked in silence to the circle of rocks that surrounded the tree of obedience. He turned and faced the brethren and the merchants. "I will leave Scetis today," he said, "and try to reach the mountain of St. Anthony before the Berbers arrive. If they kill me, God may condemn them as murderers, and close to them the door of salvation. I will not accept a crown of martyrdom at the cost of another man's soul." He paused for a time. No one moved. "Each of you may stay or go, as you will."

He turned to the merchants. "I would ask that you take two or three of the brethren with you, and that you stop at the monastery of Abba Macarius on your way out of the valley. Go to the house of the women and take with you as many as will leave. Take them to Amma Sarah, who has a house near the Nile."

The merchants agreed.

"The rest of you: pray that you have the courage to leave quickly, or to die well," Abba John said. Then he walked back to his cell and began to gather the things he would take with him when he left.

Abba John, Daniel, Peter, and the other monks from Scetis settled on the mountain of St. Anthony. As time passed, they learned from travelers that the Berbers had not cut down the tree of obedience, and that its fruit was still sweet. Yet Abba John did not return to Scetis while he lived. He died in peace on the mountain of St. Anthony.

St. John the Little

St. John is remembered as St. John the Dwarf in the Latin tradition, and St. John the Little or St. John the Short in the Greek and Coptic traditions.

While animal companions show up in many saints' stories, there is nothing in any source materials that suggests that St. John had a fennec fox as an animal companion. There is a fragment of a Coptic life, however, that gives him a crocodile as a companion. Because crocodiles are ill-suited to life in the desert, and because St. John was small, I rather liked the idea of him having a small animal as his companion.

In the Roman Empire during the 4th and 5th centuries, widows and other women who controlled their own property often chose to provide for the needs of monks, priests, and bishops. Some of these women, like Paësia, gave so generously that they fell into debt, at which point the Roman Code allowed their creditors to force them to work as prostitutes until they paid off their debt.

This situation became so common that, in 370 AD, the emperors Valentinian, Valens, and Gratian decided something had to be done to protect these pious women. They issued a decree forbidding widows from giving anything to clerics or monks, and forbidding clerics and monks from visiting widows. Emperor Marcian lifted these restrictions in 455, and in 465, Emperor Severus reinstated them.

Prayer
You have become a star of light upon the earth, O blessed and holy one, my master and father Abba John. Through your humility and angelic life, you made Scetis like the stars. You became a harbor of salvation, you have raised the dead, you have exorcised the demons, and you have healed the sick. Pray to the Lord on our behalf, O my master and father, Abba John the Little, that He may forgive us our sins.

St. Nicholas of Myra
Born March 15, 270, Patara, Lycia
Died December 6, 343, Myra, Lycia

FEAST DAY: DECEMBER 6

"There's a bed in the attic," the innkeeper said. "If you want a bed to yourself, your grace, I'm afraid that's the best we can do."

"Thank you," said Bishop Nicholas. "As long as the attic has a bed and a basin of water, I won't need anything more."

The innkeeper picked up a lantern. "Follow men, then," he said. Bishop Nicholas rose stiffly from the bench and followed the innkeeper through a narrow hall and up a flight of stairs. As they reached the top, the innkeeper said, "Watch your head." Bishop Nicholas ducked through the door to the attic. The walls were lined with crocks and barrels. Smoked meat and onions and herbs hung from the rafters.

A washbasin sat upside down on a small table. The innkeeper set the lantern down and turned the basin right side up, then walked to the window and opened the shutters. He stood with his back to the bishop, staring out the window. Nicholas waited in silence. Finally, the innkeeper spoke. "I set this room up for my brother, who was a deacon in Xanthos when the persecutions began. When they ended, and he was released from prison, it seemed that he left some part of himself behind. It troubled him during the night, calling out to him in his sleep."

"Your brother, where is he now?"

"He is at rest with God, your grace." The innkeeper turned back towards Bishop Nicholas. "The bed is there. I'll have my boy bring water. Will you be needing anything else?"

"This will do, my good man. Thank you."

The innkeeper gave a slight bow and ducked through the door. Bishop Nicholas walked to the window and stared out into the darkness, looking beyond the courtyard and into the past. When he came back to himself, he closed the shutters. He wondered briefly when the boy would bring water, then realized that a jug and a linen towel had appeared on the table next to the basin. He washed his hands and face, chanted his prayers, and went wearily to bed.

Nicholas slept, and his sleep was filled with dreams of flickering shadows and the shouting of guards, the sounds of blows, the screams of men echoing in the night. A guard in the dream knocked a young deacon to the floor, the deacon from Xanthos. Bishop Nicholas pushed the guard. The guard stumbled, caught his balance, then turned and hit Nicholas square in the face with the butt of his spear. Pain exploded across Nicholas's face as his bones shattered. Blood ran down his cheeks and in his mouth. He tried to scream, but he couldn't pull the air into his lungs. He couldn't breathe.

As he turned his head and raised his arms to avoid another blow, he heard his name. The guards never said his name.

He opened his eyes and put his hands on his face. There was no blood. He wasn't in prison. He was at the inn. The dream was gone. He was awake. Yet there was still shouting. It was coming from the courtyard. He heard his name again. Someone needed him. He pushed himself up from the bed, went to the window, and threw open the shutters. "Who calls me?" he shouted into the confusion below.

It had taken time to calm things down and get the story. Too much time. A rider had come from Myra. Eustathius, the governor, had accepted a bribe, a chest of gold, to have three men arrested, tried, convicted, and executed before Bishop

Nicholas returned. Eustathius could make up any crime he wanted, use the gold to procure false witnesses and pay judges. Any gold remaining after the execution would be his to keep.

The love of gold was stronger in Eustathius than the fear of God. He took the gold.

The trial had ended before the seventh hour. When the verdict was announced, the rider borrowed a good horse from a good man and rode through the day and the night to find Bishop Nicholas and summon him back to Myra.

The execution was set for the first hour of the morning.

"I'll leave now," Bishop Nicholas said. "With the help of God, I may get there in time."

"Not on your mule you won't," said the innkeeper. "He's a good beast, and if you ask him to, he'll walk all night and all day tomorrow to get you home. That's just it, you see? By the time your mule gets you there, the men will be dead and buried."

Bishop Nicholas rubbed his forehead above the bridge of his nose. He needed the pain to stop so he could think. "Is there someone in the village with a horse I can borrow?" he asked.

The innkeeper nodded. "The lord Theodore has a villa just over the hill. He loves his horses more than he loves his children. I'll send one of my boys to tell him that you have need of his best horse."

"A man who loves his horses that well won't send his best horse," said Bishop Nicholas. "I'll take whatever he is willing to send. Just make sure your boy knows to get it here quickly."

Bishop Nicholas and the innkeeper were still in the courtyard when the boy rode up. The horse was gray, with large eyes and a narrow muzzle. "It seems I was wrong about the lord Theodore," the bishop said.

The boy dismounted. "The lord Theodore sends this horse to his grace, the Bishop Nicholas," he said. "He said you should know that, while this horse is small, it is truly his best horse. It is as fast as the wind, as intelligent as a man, with the courage of a lion and the stamina of an ox. It has carried the lord Theodore to war, and it will carry you wherever you need to go."

Bishop Nicholas nodded. "My father once had such a horse." He rubbed the horse's neck, whispered in his ear. The horse whickered. "Can someone help me mount?" he asked. "My back, you know."

The innkeeper cupped his hands and helped the bishop onto the horse. "Godspeed," he said.

Bishop Nicholas turned the horse towards Myra. The road was good, the moon was full, and the horse was one that a man might dream of riding. By the grace of God, this horse might get him there in time.

Bishop Nicholas was dozing in the saddle when the birds began to sing their morning praises. The stars were fading; the moon was low in the west. He overtook a farmer heading towards Myra with a heavy wagon and asked for news.

"Three executions are scheduled this morning, your grace," the farmer replied cheerfully. "The market will be crowded. I hope to have good fortune at the market today, and to return home tonight with a heavy purse and an empty wagon."

"With the help of God, man, there will be no executions today," Bishop Nicholas said. "Stop your cart and pray that I'll not be too late."

As the farmer stammered a response, Bishop Nicholas rode on. The constant motion, the lack of sleep, were making his pain worse.

That didn't matter, though. The only thing that mattered was getting to Myra in time to save three lives.

As the city grew near, the road filled with crowds pushing toward the execution field. He spoke to his horse, urging him to speed. The horse understood. His trot turned into a gallop, and the crowd parted before him like water before the prow of a ship.

The three prisoners had already been brought forth, their heads covered with linen hoods. As the men were pushed to the ground and the executioner unsheathed his sword, Bishop Nicholas turned the horse toward the executioner and bellowed, "In the name of God, I command you: Stop!"

For a moment, time itself may have stopped. The horse reared. Bishop Nicholas slid from his back and landed on his feet. Three steps, and he had his hands on the executioner's sword. He wrested it away and threw it to the ground.

"There will be no killing today."

Eustathius, the governor, was absent from vigil on Saturday, and absent from the Divine Liturgy on Sunday. On Wednesday, he came to see

Bishop Nicholas privately. They talked past the time of supper and well into the night.

When Eustathius returned to church many weeks later, he stood with the penitents, outside the nave. But he came. He kept coming, until Bishop Nicholas granted him absolution and restored him to his former place.

What became of the chest of gold? Perhaps Eustathius gave it to the men he'd meant to kill. Perhaps Bishop Nicholas told him to distribute every bit of it as alms before he dared to set foot inside the Church again. There's no way to know. Penance is a private matter.

But the story of what happened on the execution field became widely known. Those wrongly accused would call on Bishop Nicholas, even when he was far away, and he would come to their aid. There are those who say that he still comes to the aid of people who call on him today.

St. Nicholas of Myra

Italian sailors stole the relics of St. Nicholas from the tomb in Myra in 1087 and took them to Bari, Italy. A cathedral was built there, and when it was completed in 1089, St. Nicholas's bones were placed in a tomb in the crypt. They lay undisturbed until May 5, 1953. At that time, the crypt that contained St. Nicholas's tomb needed extensive repairs. During the repairs, St. Nicholas's bones had to be removed from the tomb for safety.

When the bones were removed, and again just before they were reinterred, they were examined, measured, and photographed. From the bones, we learned that St. Nicholas was not quite 5 feet 6 inches tall (an average height for a man at the time), that he was slender, and that his diet was largely vegetarian. We also learned that he had severe arthritis in his spine and pelvis, and that his nose had been quite badly broken. It had healed crooked, and his skull had thickened in a way that would have caused chronic head pain.

Prayer

Rejoice, O holy hierarch Nicholas, most sacred mind, pure abode of the Trinity, pillar of the Church, confirmation of the faithful, helper of the afflicted, star who with the brilliant rays of your right acceptable prayers ever dispels the darkness of trial and tribulation, calm haven where the imperiled who flee to you are saved from the threefold waves of life! Entreat Christ God, that He send down upon our souls great mercy.

St. Odilia of Alsace

Born 660, Alsace, Austrasia, Kingdom of the Franks
Died 720, Alsace, Austrasia, Kingdom of the Franks

FEAST DAY DECEMBER 13

Adalrich, Duke of Alsace, paced outside the birthing chamber. His wife, Berswinde, was about to birth her first son. He could hear the soft sounds of the harp and the murmurs of the midwives as his wife moaned and screamed. The baby, his son, would soon arrive.

Soon, all inside the room was quiet, save for the sound of the harp. From time to time, Adalrich would stop pacing to listen. How long could it possibly take? Was something amiss?

Eventually, the door to the chamber opened a crack. "Your grace, you may come in," said the midwife.

Adalrich entered. The room was warm. The only light came from a small fire in a brazier. "Let me see my son!" he said. Berswinde flinched. Her hair was wet with sweat. She was holding the swaddled baby to her breast.

"My lord husband," she said.

"Let me see him!"

"My lord husband," she said. "You have a daughter."

Adalrich's eyes narrowed. "A daughter?" he said. "A daughter?"

"Yes, my lord husband. A daughter."

"Well, let me see her, then," he said.

Berswinde unlatched the babe from her breast and turned her towards her father.

He stared at her, then turned to the midwives. "What's wrong with her eyes?" he asked in a voice that was uncharacteristically soft. The harp fell silent.

"She is blind, my lord."

"Blind?" he repeated. Then, louder, "Blind? By God, whose fault is it, that a child of mine is born blind?"

Berswinde took a deep breath. "There is no fault, my lord husband. When the holy disciples asked our Lord Jesus who had sinned that a man was born blind, Jesus said, 'Neither this man nor his parents sinned, but that God's works might be revealed in him.'"

"I won't have it. I will not have a blind child.

Better that she be stillborn."

"My lord husband, she is not stillborn. Look at her. She breathes. She suckles."

"She is dead." He turned to the midwives. "Kill her, and I will tell our people that she was born dead."

"No, husband! No! You must not."

He looked at Berswinde, his eyes filled with rage. "Must not? Are you my wife?"

Her voice trembled as she answered. "I am your wife, and you are my husband and my lord."

"Is my word not your law?"

"Yes, my lord husband," she said. "Your word is my law. Yet you must forgive me, for I would not have you cross God's law and come to perdition."

Adalrich clenched his fists. His jaw tightened. He spoke slowly, practically spitting out each word. "I will not have a blind child."

The babe began to whimper. "My lord husband," said Berswinde, "we can give the child to my servant here and have her take the child away. She can get a wet nurse. She can raise the child. We will say the child was born dead. No one will know."

"I should kill you and the child both," he said. He turned and walked to the door, then stopped. "Send the child away," he said, with his back to the room. "Send her away. Just make sure I never hear a word of her, or she will surely die."

Before long, people were talking about the blind child the servant was fostering, and speculating about whose child it might be. Berswinde heard the rumors, and for a moment she couldn't breathe. Her husband had only just had his men kill Abbot Germanus of Grandval in a fit of pique when negotiations had not gone his way. He would not hesitate to kill their daughter if the rumors reached his ears.

She sent for a page. "I need you to deliver a private message for me. Go to the convent at Palma, and talk to my aunt, the abbess. Tell her that God will send a blind child to her convent, and that she must take this child in, and teach her to pray and to give alms and to please God." The boy repeated the message back to her. "Yes, that's right. Now go, quickly, and do not let anyone know where you are going."

When the first page was gone, she called

for another. She smiled when she recognized the boy. "I need you to deliver a message to a woman in the village where your mother lives. The woman has a foster child, a girl, who is blind. Ask your mother to take you to the woman. Tell the woman to take the child to the convent at Palma, and hand her over to the abbess. After you have delivered the message, you may spend the rest of the day and tomorrow with your mother."

Once both messages were on their way, she retired to the chapel to pray.

The abbess of Palma accepted the child without question. The convent educated many girls of noble birth. One more wasn't difficult, even if the one was blind.

Years passed. The blind girl learned how to spin a fine thread. She memorized the Psalms and the Gospels. She chanted the hours of prayer. She studied the lives of the saints. She assisted the nuns who distributed alms to the poor. She loved the nuns who looked after her, and they returned that love.

When the girl was 12 years old, or maybe 13, Erhard, Bishop of Ratisbonne, was at the monastery at Regensburg. While he was praying in his cell, a voice came from everywhere and nowhere, filling the room. "Go to the convent of Palma," the Voice said. "There you will find a maiden who was born blind. Baptize her in the name of the Father, and of the Son, and of the Holy Spirit. When you anoint her with chrism, she will see the light of the sun."

Bishop Erhard was a missionary priest, accustomed to travelling. He immediately got up from his prayers and prepared for the journey. The days were fair, the trees were green, and roses and foxglove bloomed along the edge of the woods. He would need nothing more than his vestments and liturgical items, a blanket, bread, cheese, and a few coins to buy food for the way home. If he borrowed one of the monastery's horses, he could get to the convent of Palma in less than a fortnight.

He was only halfway to the convent when he encountered his dear friend and brother bishop, Hidulf of Trier. "Glory to God!" Hidulf shouted. "What joy to see you here!"

"Glory to God!" Erhard responded. "What brings you here, my brother?"

"I had a vision from God our King, telling me that you were going to the convent of Palma, to baptize a maiden, and that I should go with you."

"Did God tell you that the maiden is blind?"

"No, He didn't!" said Hidulf. "Is she, then?"

"That's what He told me. I suppose we'll know when we get there."

"Did he tell you the name to give her when you baptize her?"

"No, He didn't!" said Erhard. "Did He tell you?"

"Yes," said Hidulf with a smile. "She is to be named Odilia, the light of the sun."

"That fits!" said Erhard, "Because He told me that when she is baptized, she will see the light of the sun."

"Indeed. She was born blind that God's works might be revealed in her."

The two men went on their way rejoicing.

When at last they arrived at the convent of Palma, they asked the porter to bring the blind maiden to them. The porter, of course, brought the abbess.

"Who are you, and what is your business here?" she asked.

"Reverend Mother, forgive us. I am Erhard, Bishop of Ratisbonne, and this fellow is Hidulf, Bishop of Trier. God has revealed to us that you have, in your convent, a maiden who is blind. She has not been baptized, and God has sent me to baptize her."

The abbess looked at them thoughtfully. "Forgive me, your grace, but your cassock is shabby, and you look more like monks than bishops."

"Indeed, Reverend Mother, God has granted you the gift of discernment. We are monks of the monastery of Regensburg. We were consecrated bishops so that we could bring the Gospel to the pagans. But we are indeed monks."

The abbess nodded as he spoke. "God told you that there is a blind maiden here, you say?"

"Yes," said Erhard. "He did."

"A blind maiden in need of baptism," the abbess said softly to herself. "What of the girl's family?" she asked.

The two bishops looked at each other. "Did

God tell you anything about her family?" asked Erhard.

"No," said Hidulf. "I didn't know she had a family."

"What about godparents?" the abbess asked.

Hidulf looked at Erhard. "When he told you to baptize the girl, did He tell you who should be the godparents?"

"No, not a word." Erhard turned to the abbess. "Reverend Mother, I'm afraid God didn't reveal anything about godparents or family to either of us. Perhaps one of your nuns would be godmother to her? Since God sent Bishop Hidulf to join me for the baptism, perhaps he can serve as godfather? Would that suit you, Reverend Mother?"

"If you will forgive me, your grace, with your blessing I shall have my porter take your baggage to the guest house. When she has done so, I shall have her inspect your baggage to ensure that there are no weapons."

"Reverend Mother, your porter may inspect our baggage. She will find no weapons there. We are armed only with the Cross of Peace."

The next morning, before the Mass, Bishop Erhard baptized the blind maiden in the name of the Holy Trinity, giving her the name Odilia. When he anointed her eyes with the holy chrism, he said, "In the name of Our Lord Jesus Christ, may your body see as your soul does." Immediately her eyes grew wide, and she gasped. She turned her head to one side, and then the other. She blinked several times. "What do you see, my child?" asked Bishop Erhard.

"I do not know," she said, turning towards his voice. "There was a man born blind, and when Jesus anointed his eyes with spittle, he saw men like trees. I think perhaps I am like that man." She closed her eyes, then opened them. "I do not know yet what I see," she said, "but I know that I see."

The sisters sang praises to God, rejoicing that they had all been counted worthy to witness a miracle.

After the Mass, the abbess told the bishops privately who Odilia's parents were and how she had come to be a ward of the convent.

"Glory to God," said Hidulf. "Duke Adalrich will rejoice to receive his daughter back, now that God has given her sight."

The abbess shook her head. "He will not receive her back."

"But his reason for sending her away is no more. Surely his paternal affection will be restored with her sight."

"If he hears of her, he will kill her."

Hidulf found it impossible to believe that the duke would kill his own daughter, especially now that she could see. When he and Erhard left the monastery, he decided to go to Hohenburg Castle to share the news of Odilia's healing with her father.

The conversation did not go well. Duke Adalrich refused to acknowledge that he had ever had a blind daughter. As his denials grew louder, they could be heard beyond the chamber where Adalrich had received the bishop. Didon, Adalrich's son and presumptive heir, whom he had sired with a tavern wench many years ago, before he had married Berswinde, heard what was being said. He had a sister. A sister who had been visited by a miracle. A sister who could be married to secure a valuable alliance. How could his father not see that?

"I am sure everything I have said is based

on a misunderstanding," Bishop Hidulf said at last. "Scurrilous rumors. People say all kinds of things about great men like yourself. I can assure you that I will not bother you again about the maiden at the convent at Palma. She is my goddaughter, but she is nothing to you. I'm sure that we can agree that no harm should come to her because of the things that have been said today."

Duke Adalrich scowled. "No harm will come to her," he said.

Bishop Hidulf breathed a silent prayer of gratitude, and Didon breathed a great sigh of relief.

Didon got two sheets of fine vellum and sat at the large oak table near the window of the solar, where he could take advantage of the afternoon sun. As he thought through what he wanted to say, he trimmed a quill. Then he wrote two letters, one to the Lady Berswinde's aunt, the abbess of the convent of Palma, and one to Odilia. To Odilia, he expressed his joy at learning that he had a sister, his delight in her healing, and his desire to bring her home. To the abbess, he explained that he had learned of his sister Odilia from Bishop Hidulf. He didn't mention that he'd been eavesdropping, and he didn't mention his father's response. No need to complicate matters. He told the abbess that he desired to send a company of men to escort Odilia home. If he had her blessing, he asked that she read Odilia the letter addressed to her.

Didon re-read both letters. Satisfied with his work, he folded the letters together, then melted a bit of sealing wax over a candle and sealed them closed. He would have a page take them to the convent in the morning.

Didon read the letter from the abbess. "My lord Desiderius," it read. "Your sister cannot leave the monastery. Although God has taken away her blindness, she still sees dimly, as through a glass. She has learned to recognize a few objects by sight, which she formerly knew only by touch. She will learn most readily in a familiar environment. For that reason, I must decline your kind offer to bring her home to your family."

Didon wrote the abbess again, and again, and again. She responded kindly and firmly each time. Neither he nor the abbess mentioned Odilia's father, of course. They only discussed Odilia, her vision, and her ability to manage ordinary things like eating and dressing and spinning, things she had done easily when she could not see and now struggled to do.

Weeks and months and seasons passed. Finally, the abbess agreed that Odilia might leave and be restored to her family. Then Didon had to get the master of the stables to agree to his plan. Somehow, somehow, he had to do everything without either his father or the Lady Berswinde learning of his doings.

In the late summer, six of Didon's men went out on fine horses, with two older women servants on palfreys, two pack horses, and a palfrey for Odilia.

Didon and his father were standing on the terrace when a company of men on horseback came around the curve in the steep road towards the castle. "Those look like your men," said Adalrich.

"They are," said Didon. "I sent them to the convent of Palma, to escort an honored guest to Hohenburg."

Adalrich stiffened. "Who might this guest be?" he asked.

"It is your daughter, my lord father, who was dead and is now alive. She is returning to us."

Adalrich turned to look at Didon. "I have no daughter," he said, with menace in his voice.

"My lord father, you have sons in plenty. A daughter—"

"I have no daughter," Adalrich roared. He swung his staff, hitting Didon's head with a terrible blow. Didon crumpled to the ground.

Silence swept over the terrace. Adalrich stood over his son, watching blood drip from his nose and his ear. Then he turned to the nearest servant. "What are you standing there for?" he shouted. "Go fetch the doctor. Now!"

Within moments, the terrace was filled with people. The castle doctor arrived. Servants bustled in and out. Berswinde came onto the terrace, then stood as still as if she were stone. Her sons stood with her. Not long after, Didon's men came in, with Odilia.

Odilia didn't know any of the people on the terrace, except the men who had escorted her from the convent. She turned to the one called Peyre and asked who was lying injured on the ground. "That, my lady," he said, "is your brother Didon."

"Didon!" she cried. She ran to him and knelt beside him. In her years at the convent, she had learned prayers for the healing of soul and body, and so she began to pour out the prayers with many tears. As the tears fell on Didon, he began to stir. As she pronounced the Amen, he sat up and looked around.

"Odilia?" he said, as if he were in a dream.

"Yes, Didon! I am here!"

"Odilia! Father, my Lady Berswinda. Behold, my sister, your daughter! Odilia is here!"

"I have no daughter!" Adalrich bellowed. Odilia cowered back from him, and Didon wrapped his arms protectively around her.

"Get her out of my sight! I want her out! Out!"

Odilia stood up. She looked around to get her bearings, then ran back through the castle as she had come in, down the road and into the woods. She kept running until she was thoroughly lost. She stopped to rest, then got up and ran some more. Eventually, she found herself making her way along a narrow path with a cliff on one side of her and a ravine on the other. A river flowed fast and loud in the bottom of the ravine. She stopped again. Over the sound of the river came the sounds of men and horses in the distance. If they followed her path, she would have nowhere to go.

She signed herself with the cross. She had no idea which way was east so she began to pray where she stood. "Lord, how are they increased that trouble me! Many are they that rise up against me. Many are they that say of my soul, there is no help for him in God. But You, O Lord, are my shield and my glory; You are the lifter of my head. I cried to the Lord with my voice, and He heard me from His holy mountain."

As she said those words, she saw a dark stripe on the face of the cliff and realized that it was an opening. "Salvation belongs to the Lord," she cried softly. "Your blessing is upon Your people."

She ducked her head and slipped through the opening into the cave. The darkness enveloped her like a familiar friend. She walked back in the cave as far as she could. There, she found a dry rock shelf, knelt beside it, and prayed.

Adalrich and his men came down the path single file. They walked past Odilia's cave without seeing the narrow gap in the rock.

"That trollop had to have come this way,"

said Adalrich. "Could she have crossed the river?"

"Perhaps farther ahead," said one of the men. "There's a shallow ford perhaps two miles hence, where she could cross. Along this way, though, she'd risk breaking her neck to get down to the river."

As he spoke, a sound of movement came from the cliff above them. One of the horses whinnied. A few small rocks bounced down the cliff face and fell among them.

"Is there a place where she could have scrambled up the cliff?" asked Adalrich.

"Not unless she's a goat," said another, to raucous laughter.

A larger rock loosed itself from the cliffside, bounced against a tree that had fastened itself precariously to the rocks, hit the path, careened down the slope, and landed in the river with a splash. The horses twitched their ears.

"Well, then, is a goat up there pushing rocks at us?" asked Adalrich.

At the sound of his voice, the section of the cliff above them began to come apart. Adalrich's horse reared. The rocks began tumbling down on them. More rocks, and larger, followed them, striking the men and the horses. As the face of the cliff began to collapse, the men turned their horses and rode back the way they had come.

The thunder of the rockfall slowly faded. There were no more sounds of men or horses, only the soft sounds of the river and small creatures that move in darkness. Odilia stayed on her knees by the rock shelf, chanting the Psalter through the night. When the morning light began to brighten the entrance to the cave, she said her amen and ventured out.

The rockslide blocked the path beyond her cave. She listened to the birds and the trees and the river. She realized that she needed water. There was no path to the river here. Crossing herself, she said, "Cause me to hear Your mercy in the morning, for I trust in you. Cause me to know the way I should walk, for I lift my soul to You."

At that moment, a bright sound appeared behind her. She turned. A spring was bubbling from the cliff wall between her cave and the rock fall. The spring had not been there when she went into the cave, and it had not been there when she stepped out of the cave. She would have heard it. She knelt down, saying, "He sends springs into the valleys, which run among the hills. He waters the hills from His chambers. The earth is satisfied with the fruit of Your works." Then she drank from the spring.

Now what? God had provided the cave and the spring. Where would He have her go now? The castle was out of the question. Could she find her way to the convent?

As she stood there, thinking, a man walked silently down the path towards her. "My lady," he said. She jumped back as if he were a wild animal, and then she recognized him. It was the man who was called Peyre.

"My lady, my lord Didon, your brother, has sent me to find you and bring you home."

"To Palma?" she asked.

"To Hohenburg," he said.

"I will not go there. The duke will kill me."

"My lady, my lord Didon and my lord Adalrich have come to an understanding. You are to come to Hohenburg." Odilia didn't move. She didn't speak. "My lady, by my life, you will be safe at Hohenburg."

"My life is in God's hands," she said. "I will go with you."

As Odilia and Peyre walked towards the castle gate, Didon and Berswinde rushed out to greet her. They fell on Odilia with kisses and tears. Thanking God and Peyre for her safe return, they led her through the gate and through the castle to the guest chamber.

Odilia stood just inside the richly furnished chamber. Two large windows in the south wall opened into alcoves, filling them with light. The rest of the room was dark and cool. On a table, candles flickered, and in their light Odilia could see plates of candied ginger and other confections, and glasses, and a flagon of wine.

She walked around the room silently, running her hands along the walls and the furnishings. There was a second door on the east side of the room. She looked at her mother. "Where does this go?" she asked.

"Your servants are quartered there," she said. "Your clothing and jewels will be stored there."

"My lady mother," Odilia said, "I have no servants, nor clothing beyond what I am wearing, and no jewels."

"You are my daughter," Berswinde told her. "I have assigned four maidservants to you, and I will see that you have clothing and jewels befitting your station."

"Does my lord father know I am here?" she asked.

"He knows," said Didon, pouring wine. "He has accepted you here as his honored guest."

"He requires only one thing of you," said Berswinde. "He wants you to stay out of his sight."

"Oh, he will not see me!" said Odilia. She looked at the table, with the wine and the sweets. "Where will I take my meals?" she asked. "Will I sit with the servants in the great hall?"

"You will eat here, in your chamber," said Didon. He handed her a glass of wine. "I will join you for your meals today. Other days, the twins Haicho and Adalrich the younger will dine with you. They are not quite a year younger than you. Little Adalbart, the youngest of our brothers, will join you from time to time, if you can abide his childish antics."

"I must eat in the hall with my lord husband," Berswinde said. She paused and stared at the candles for a time before turning back to Odilia. "My daughter, my child, you are not a prisoner, and you will not eat alone."

Over the next days and weeks, Odilia got to know her brothers. They explained their father's habits, so she could stay out of his sight. They shared meals in her chamber. The twins played the rebec and flute for her. Didon sang songs that she had never heard at Palma, and she sang songs of the saints for him. When the weather was fine, they walked with her around the castle and its grounds, and through the woods and fields beyond.

As she explored further, she asked her brother about the large shapes that were clustered near the roads and fields. "Those are the huts that shelter the serfs who belong to this land," Didon explained. The people near the huts were thin, their clothes ragged.

When she woke that night to pray the midnight office, she felt the sorrow of the serfs, and she knew their hunger. When she rose from her prayers, she dressed herself, put on her shoes, and walked confidently through the dark halls to the kitchen. A few servants were there, singing softly as they scoured the smoke stains from the great iron pots. They looked at her in surprise as she entered.

"Please," she said, "would you pack a large basket with bread and cheese and apples?"

"My lady," said the old woman who ran the kitchen at night, "you should send your maidservants to fetch food to your room. You need not come yourself."

"Oh, the food is not for me!" said Odilia. "I am taking food to the serfs who live down the road."

A basket was quickly packed. "I'll send for Sir Peyre," said the old woman. "He and a man servant will walk with you and light your way."

"There's no need," said Odilia. "I can walk in darkness as well as in light."

Every night after her prayers, Odilia went to the kitchen. Before long, the kitchen servants had a basket waiting for her. She could slip out of the castle through the wicket gate, deliver the alms, and be back at the castle well before cock crow.

On St. Stephen's Day, a storm came with fierce winds and heavy snow. She couldn't leave the castle for two nights. On the third night, she looked out her window after prayers. The snow had stopped falling, the winds had stilled, and the full moon suffused the world with a light like the light of heaven.

She went to the kitchen. The servants had not packed a basket for her. "Please," she said, "I must go tonight."

The old woman shook her head. "It isn't safe," she said.

"God will keep me safe. I will go."

The old woman filled a basket, and Odilia went.

It took much longer that night to deliver the alms and to make her way back up the hill to the castle. Her shoes and skirt were caked with snow. Her feet were numb. As she went in through the wicket gate, she crossed herself and said, "The Lord shall preserve your going out and your coming in, from this time forth and forevermore."

When she stopped in the courtyard to shake the snow from her shoes and her skirts, she felt someone watching her. She looked around. In a dark corner was her father.

"My lord!" she said, "I didn't know you would be here. I will go to my chamber now. You will not see me again."

"Wait," he said. "I have something to say to you."

"Yes, my lord."

"The kitchen servants told me that you have been bearing alms in the night to the surrounding country folk," he said.

"Yes, my lord."

"This night, because of the storm, they were afraid for your safety. So I have waited here, to watch for your return."

Odilia didn't know what to say, so she said nothing.

"Go to your chamber now. Your maids will take your gown and get you into something warm and dry. I will have the kitchen servants bring you hot spiced wine. When it is time to break your fast, your brother Didon will come for you and bring you to the great hall."

"Yes, my lord," said Odilia. She looked up at her father, and their eyes met. It was as if they were seeing each other for the very first time.

Odilia was surprised by the sound of many voices coming from the great hall. "Is it always this loud?" she asked her brother.

"Is what always this loud?"

"The great hall."

"Oh. Yes, it's loud. With so many people, how could it be quiet?"

"In the convent," said Odilia, "the refectory is quiet. One nun reads from the scriptures or the lives of the saints, and the rest of us listen as we eat."

"We do things differently here," said Didon. "You'll grow accustomed to it."

They entered the great hall, washed their hands, and Didon led Odilia to a seat at the high table, next to her mother. He took the seat on the other side of his father.

Slowly the noise in the hall died down. Everyone, of course, knew Odilia. They knew that she had restored Didon to life by her prayers. They knew about her almsgiving. They knew that she was not to be seen in any place where Duke Adalrich might see her. Many of them had grown to love her since she had arrived at the castle. Many of them had motioned for her to leave a room or turn back from a staircase when they knew the duke might see her.

"My people," Adalrich said, "The young woman here with me is my daughter, Odilia. She lived for many years at the convent at Palma, where your lady Berswinde's aunt is the abbess. As you can see, she is now returned to us. You will accord her all honor and obedience, as is her due."

There were raucous cheers, and cries of "God save Odilia!" When those died down, the servants brought in plates of pork rissoles and pastries covered with green sauce and flagons of wine and beer, and the sounds of eating and talking and laughter filled the hall.

Odilia began spending her afternoons in the solar, rather than in her chamber. The twins often joined her there, bringing their instruments and begging her to sing for them. When the afternoon sun flooded the solar with light, her mother brought linen and silk and began teaching her the art of embroidery. When she had enough skill, Odilia wanted to embroider vestments for the altar at Palma.

Sometimes her lord father and her brother Didon joined them in the solar, to manage the accounts and correspondence for the castle.

On this day, Didon broke the seal on a letter and began to read. As he read, he began to smile. "My lord father, read this!" he said, holding out the letter.

Adalrich moved the candle a bit, to better see the parchment. On reading it, he, too, smiled. "This would make a fine alliance," he said.

"The lands and castles he suggests as the dowry are all near his lands. He could manage them as well as we."

Odilia looked up. "Who is to be wed?" she asked.

"Why, sister, there is a German prince who needs a wife. His father wants a maid who is as pious as she is beautiful, who is wise and practical and gifted in the art of healing."

"He wants you for his son," said Adalrich.

"Why – what – no, my lord father!"

Adalrich looked at her. His eyes narrowed and his jaw tightened.

"What do you mean, my daughter?"

Odilia set her embroidery aside. "I will not marry him."

"Am I not your father, Odilia?"

"You are, my lord father."

"Is it not my right to choose a husband for

you?"

"It is your right, my lord father. You may choose, but I must consent." She paused. "I do not consent."

"Odilia."

"My lord father, I want to return to Palma to take holy vows. I want to live in the convent."

"Odilia," said Didon. "Think of it. A prince!"

"Oh, my brother," Odilia said, "I have thought of it. I do not wish to be the wife of a prince. My heart longs for quiet and contemplation, for the divine services, for prayer."

As Odilia spoke, Adalrich's face turned red. A vein pulsed in his neck. "Odilia, I do not consent to send you back to Palma."

"My lord! I – "

"Odilia, silence!" Adalrich thundered. Odilia sucked in her breath. Didon froze.

Adalrich clenched and unclenched his fists as he brought himself under control. "Odilia," he said, his voice lower but still threatening, "you will not go to Palma." Odilia closed her eyes.

Adalrich took a deep breath. Didon did not move.

Finally, Adalrich shook his head, as if he were shaking off an enchantment or a dream. "I will make Hohenburg a convent," he said. "You will be the abbess."

Didon stood, took two steps towards Odilia, and placed his hands on her shoulders. Odilia opened her eyes. "My lord father?" she said.

"My daughter, God gave light to your eyes, and you brought that light here. That light burned my heart, which was full of darkness. That's why I wouldn't see you at first. But your light has overcome the darkness."

Tears began to wet Odilia's face.

"You must stay here, my daughter, on this mountain." He ran his hands through his hair. "Odilia, without your light I will not see God. I need you. Stay here. Bring your light to all of Alsace. Bring your light to me."

"Oh, my lord father," Odilia said, "my lord father, yes. To that, I consent."

St. Odilia of Alsace

St. Odilia of Alsace is sometimes conflated with St Odilia of Cologne. St. Odilia of Cologne was the daughter of a king in Britain. When she and a group of other virgins were on a pilgrimage, they were captured by Huns and martyred in Cologne in the year 304.

Our St. Odilia (or Odile, as it is sometimes written) was the first child of Berswinde of Austrasia, who was the wife of Adalrich, Duke of Alsace. Odilia had four brothers. Some sources say that her brother Hugo was struck and killed by their father, but none of her father's sons were named Hugo or Hugh. Among Adalrich's sons was Didon, or Desiderion, about whom little is known. He was likely older than Odilia, born before Adalrich married Berswinde, so it seems to me likely that he was the one sometimes called Hugo.

There is no longer a convent at Hohenburg. The monastic buildings are now a hotel and retreat center and a café. The church, however, is still an active Roman Catholic parish, and the relics of St. Odilia are still there.

Prayer

Lord, our Father, You gave Saint Odilia the grace to see and to believe. By her prayer and the power of the Holy Spirit, open our eyes to see what is good and beautiful in the world and in our brothers and sisters, and grant that we may behold them with the gaze of love in which You never cease to behold us, your children.

St. Thorlak of Iceland
Born 1133, Fljotshlith, Iceland
Died 1193, Skálaholt, Iceland

FEAST DAY DECEMBER 23

Gizurr Hallsson stared past the young men who were shoveling earth into Thorlak's grave. The sky was covered with featureless clouds. The light seemed to come from everywhere and nowhere. The voices chanting the prayers washed over him like the sound of the wind or the ocean. Bishop Thorlak was gone. He felt as he had when his parents had died. Orphaned. Alone.

He took a deep breath and looked around. He wasn't alone. Priest Páll, Bishop Thorlak's sister-son, was there, along with many other eminent men. They all seemed to be standing alone. Gizurr remembered the words that Bishop Thorlak had said to comfort him when his father had died, that the death of a holy man was glorious, because all good men would rather be by his side in death than by the side of many men still living.

He thought of his ancestors. They didn't keep their dead by their side. They buried those they loved at the very edges of their farmsteads as far away as they could. Their dead were buried facing away from their homes, so they could not look on the living. How strange those ideas seemed now. His father was buried here, on the south side of the church, with all the men who had died here since their families were baptized a century ago. Bishop Thorlak and the leper would join them, and when he came to the church to pray, he would walk by them and remember them.

He pulled his cloak closer around himself. The young men had begun closing the grave of the leper that Bishop Thorlak had taken from poverty and had cared for as a brother. The leper, alone of all of them, had gone with Bishop Thorlak in death. Both had died the day before Christmas Eve. He had seen their bodies then, and all the injuries and wounds and scars of this life were gone. Their skin was as smooth and clear as a baby's. There was no smell of sickness or death in the room, but rather a fragrance that made him think of thyme blooming in the spring.

He had helped prepare their bodies for burial and had helped carry them into the church. He himself had cut Bishop Thorlak's hair and given it to Priest Páll. Priest Páll would give locks of hair to those who mourned the death of Bishop Thorlak, to comfort them in their grief.

Gizurr realized that he no longer heard the sound of shovels and earth, nor the voice of the priest. Everyone was looking at him, waiting for him to speak. He pulled his thoughts back to himself. He was the lawspeaker. Today, he would speak of Bishop Thorlak, his lord and his friend.

He began by speaking of all the bishops who had ruled over Skálaholt before Thorlak's day, placing Bishop Thorlak in the proper context of the Church. Then he reminded his listeners of Thorlak's childhood.

"It was fitting that God chose Thorhallr and Halla as Bishop Thorlak's parents. They were righteous people, from good families, with eminent ancestors. In Thorlak's birth, the words of the King and Prophet David were fulfilled, that the kindred of the righteous would be blessed.

"Thorhallr and Halla were blessed with many children, but with little wealth. In the year that some of you will still remember, the year the ocean yielded no fish, they faced a winter of hunger. To ensure that they all survived that terrible winter, Thorhallr and Halla divided their children between them and left their farm near the Seljalandsfoss waterfall. Each took refuge with other members of their families, because of their poverty.

"This was a cause of grief for the family. Yet what the evil one meant for evil, God meant for good. Halla took refuge in Oddi, and the priest Eyjolfr Samundarson became a foster father to young Thorlak. The Priest Eyjolfr could see that Thorlak was not like other boys. He preferred silence to speech. He loved rules and patterns, and if his mother or his priest could show him the pattern, he would follow it faithfully." A smile played around the corner of Gizurr's mouth. "If he could not see the pattern, if he did not know the point of what he was asked to do, he would not do it.

"When other boys engaged in rough games or bawdiness or athletic contests, Thorlak preferred to stay home with his mother. Halla taught him to read, and books became his true joy. Although Thorlak was young, the Priest Eyjolfr saw in him the beginning of wisdom. Householders and chiefs saw Thorlak's wisdom as well, and they would come to him for counsel, as if he were an elder.

"When Thorlak was but 15 years old, the Priest Eyjolfr asked Bishop Magnus to ordain him to the diaconate, and the bishop agreed. From that time on, Thorlak would chant the appointed prayers each day, according to the rule given him by the bishop. Between times of prayer he would read and write. If there was time left over, he would learn his genealogy and family history from his mother.

"Bishop Magnus died later that year, and the see was orphaned, as it is now." Gizurr took a deep breath and swallowed hard. One of the men standing between Thorlak's grave and the grave of the leper rubbed his mittened hand across his face. "Without a bishop," Gizurr continued, and his voice caught. He paused, then started again. "Without a bishop, we had no new priests, no new deacons. Finally, our people sent to Bishop Bjorn and asked him to come to the Althing and ordain clerics for us. It was, at that time, three years since Thorlak had been made a deacon. Bishop Bjorn knew both his age and his way of life, and he chose to dispense with the canonical requirements. He ordained Thorlak a priest, along with many others.

"Thorlak took charge of several small parishes, and he was a most attentive priest. The patterns of prayer, of feasts and fasts, of divine services were a true joy for him. He took care that services were celebrated faithfully. Because he always struggled with his voice, and often found it painful to speak, he ministered to the needs of his people with wisdom and good counsel rather than with many words.

"Yet Thorlak himself felt that he lacked the education he needed to be the priest he wanted to be. He went abroad, first to Paris, and then to Lincoln, in England. He studied for six years, and when he had learned what he needed to know, he returned to Iceland.

"All who knew him rejoiced at his return, especially his mother and his sisters. He rejoiced in seeing them, and he gave them gifts. Yet his heart broke when he learned that his sister Ragnheithr had become the concubine of Jón Loptsson, who was already the wealthiest and most powerful man in all of Iceland. Thorlak, being only a priest, could not command obedience of Jón and Ragnheithr, but this relationship persuaded him that the greatest task of his ministry would be to teach his people the meaning and value of marriage."

A slight westerly wind, as gentle as a breath, began to blow, and bits of blue appeared between the clouds.

"Our beloved Bishop Thorlak, of course, never married. When he was a young priest, his family and friends encouraged him to marry a worthy widow. That was allowed in those days, although our Holy Father in Rome no longer allows priests to marry widows. Thorlak would have married, had he not received a visitor in a dream, who told him that God had other plans for him.

"The first of these plans was his friendship with the Priest Bjarnhethinn, who led the farmstead called Kirkjuber. Bjarnhethinn was older than Thorlak in years, but the two were of one age in wisdom and counsel, and they were of one mind and one soul, as Luke said of the holy apostles. Every weakness that either had was matched by a strength in the other, and so they ministered together for the benefit of all. It was said of them that, by their words and their examples, they lit up the path of mercy that leads to eternal joy.

"At Kirkjuber, Thorlak and Bjarnhethinn delighted in keeping their rule of prayer. They delighted in stories and songs, in conversations with wise men, and in all innocent pleasures except games, for Thorlak believed that gaming was never entirely innocent, and that no good could come of it.

"After six years, a man named Thorkell was dying. He had no children, so he gave his money to his kinfolk, and he told Thorlak that he wanted to give him his land so that he might form a monastery there. Thorlak wanted with all his heart to say yes. He had heard the word of the Lord calling him to give up all his possessions and to serve God alone with a pure heart. Yet he could not say yes or no without first talking to the other half of his heart, Priest Bjornhethinn.

"Priest Bjornhethinn told him that it would be a sad day for him when Thorlak left, but he could see that God had ordained this plan for the salvation of many. So Thorlak left Kirkjuber to found a monastery in Ver, on the land that Thorkell gave him. For the rest of his life, Bjornhethinn said that Thorlak's chamber at Kirkjuber would never be as well occupied as it had been when Thorlak was there, unless Thorlak should return to it. Thorlak said that he had never been so happy in his life has he had been in his years at Kirkjuber.

"As abbot of Ver, Thorlak was at once the gentlest of leaders, and the most strict. He taught the brothers to understand that the Son of God was with them always, because when two or three gathered in his name, he was there. So, he told them, it was essential that they maintain love and concord, serving others with good works in silence or with wholesome speech.

"The first of the miracles that God worked through Thorlak's hands happened when he was Abbot of Ver. No one spoke of the miracles, though, because God, through the Holy Scriptures, said that it is not right to praise a man in his lifetime, but to praise and magnify him after his life." Gizurr looked at the men standing before him, and his gaze caught each of them. "As it is now after his life, it is fitting that we praise him."

Gizurr was silent for what felt like a long time. "He was the gentlest of men, and he did not want to quench a smoking wick. If he knew that you had transgressed, and he always knew, he preferred not to rebuke you, but to let his own goodness draw you to righteousness. It was not by his words that he taught me that I should not keep a concubine. It was by the good works that he did, to protect and honor the marriages of the men and women he served." He had not realized, until that moment, that he was going to speak of himself, of what Thorlak had done for him. He wasn't entirely sure what else he should say. He looked at the sky, which had cleared and was beginning to turn the dark blue of twilight.

"You all know the story of how Bishop Kloenger, when he became ill, asked that a new bishop be chosen to replace him. Thorlak was chosen, and took up residence in Skálaholt, serving as bishop elect alongside Bishop Kloenger. He wanted to go to Norway, to be confirmed as Bishop by King Magnus, but his friends advised him that it was too dangerous at that time to travel, because of wars and hostilities. So he waited, but when Bishop Kloenger died, he said he would wait no longer. Had not St. Paul himself said that one should not tremble in fear of wicked men? So he left, and after many adventures he was consecrated Bishop of Skálaholt, and returned to us.

"For fifteen years our holy Bishop Thorlak served God and served all of us. He taught his priests to read and to perform the services with due care. Those priests who could not learn from his example, he admonished with kindness. Those who could not learn from his kind words, he spoke to with stern words tempered with mercy.

"For the rest of us, he asked us to be imitators of him, as he was an imitator of Christ, and of St. Paul and St. Nicholas. That is why he taught us to fast on the eve of the feasts of the Holy Apostles and of St. Nicholas. He especially wanted us to follow the example of St. Nicholas and reverence the poor and lowly. Bishop Thorlak washed the feet of the poor, and tended them in sickness, and met their material needs from his treasury. He wanted us to do the same.

"He required all men, even the powerful, to love their wives as Christ loves the Church, and when men failed at that, as I had failed, he required them to pay fines as their penance. Those fines did not go into the general treasury, but he used them to ensure that families would not be broken by poverty, as his own family had been. He told men that sinned against their wives that, when their treasure went to preserve the marriages of the poor, their hearts would return to their own marriages.

"So it was for me. When I saw the esteem that Bishop Thorlak had for wives, and the pity he had for concubines, my heart was broken. I had thought that my concubine had come to me freely, as a free woman. Bishop Thorlak made me see how little freedom she had, and how much I owed her because of that. I gave her a portion of my wealth when I sent her away, so that she would not be impoverished because of me, and I gave my heart back to my wife, and began to love her as Christ loves the Church.

"It wasn't just me. Other men, men of power and rank and dignity, also learned to value their own wives because our holy Bishop Thorlak valued them." Gizurr looked down at Thorlak's grave to avoid looking at Priest Páll as he said these words. Priest Páll was the son of Jón Loptsson and his concubine, Thorlak's sister, Ragnheithr.

Yet Priest Páll looked at him. "My uncle, my bishop, my lord Thorlak also taught my father these things," he said quietly. "These are things that every Christian man must know and do." Gizurr looked up and into Priest Páll's eyes. A silence, rich and pure, flowed between them.

Gizurr closed his eyes for a few moments before he spoke again. "Bishop Thorlak took seriously God's admonition that some kinds of demonic temptations could be overcome only with prayer and fasting. He fasted strictly, eating only fish and vegetables, and then only small amounts. He relaxed his fast only when he was sick. It seemed that he was always sick, from the day he became bishop, so that God's strength could be made manifest in his weakness. When he was sick, if the person tending him in his illness bade him eat cheese or eggs or meat, he would, in humility, eat what he was given.

"He consoled the sorrowful, comforted the afflicted, and reconciled enemies. He guided those who erred with meekness and mild penances, and he taught them the joy of repentance. But those who would not heed his words, he would, if he must, place them under edict of excommunication.

"Two years ago, when he was so sick that we all thought he would die, he decreed that anyone he had placed under any kind of punishment or ban would be forgiven at his death. He said this to comfort them. When he recovered, though, they argued with him, telling him that he should forgive them even though he hadn't died, and that the forgiveness he'd offered meant that he knew he was too harsh. Of course he wasn't too harsh. It was impossible for Bishop Thorlak to be harsh. Yet he told us, during his final illness, that this time, anyone who had not been reconciled to him and to the church through the penances he had ordained before his death would not be forgiven by him, but they would have to wait for the next bishop, whenever that might be."

The sky was clear and dark; the winter sun had gone, and the wind had picked up. The men standing at Thorlak's grave were cold and restless.

"I have little more to say," Gizurr assured them. "I have been with our blessed Bishop

Thorlak for the last three months. He ensured that the finances of the see were in order, then he gave gifts and bequests to his family and to the poor. He received the sacrament of the sick a week before his death, and he exchanged forgiveness with all.

"Then I said – and yet I don't think I spoke, but perhaps the Holy Spirit prompted me to speak. I asked Bishop Thorlak to stay with us after he died, and to continue to be a spiritual father to us, now and always. I told him that, when he is with God in the eternal kingdom, he will have the power to intercede on our behalf, asking God to show us mercy.

"Those who were standing in the room as I spoke these words began to weep, and Bishop Thorlak comforted us." He looked up to blink back tears. The northern sky was full of stars, with ribbons and curtains of blue and green dancing above the church. "He would not say that he would be with God after he died, but he told us that he knew with certainty that he would not be in hell.

"So I believe, so we believe, that he will always be with us, praying for us, as long as we breathe, as long as there are stars in the sky."

St. Thorlak of Iceland

This story is based on the first half of *The Saga of Bishop Þorlákr*, which includes portions of the funeral oration that was delivered by Gizurr Hallson, the elderly and venerable lawspeaker. The Saga was composed during the life of Thorlak's sister-son and successor, Bishop Páll Jónsson, and is sometimes attributed to him. From the saga, we know that Thorlak learned to read as a very young child, that he was what we might call socially awkward, and that he often found it difficult to speak. Some have concluded from these and other details of his life that he may have been autistic. He also had some form of chronic illness that was at times severe enough that he needed people to care for him.

In Iceland during St. Thorlak's time, marriage was a complex financial arrangement negotiated between families of relatively equal financial and social status. The woman's consent was not required.

Consent was required, though, for a free woman to become a concubine. Further, while a woman could not marry someone of higher standing, a poor woman (such as Bishop Thorlak's sister) could be the concubine of a wealthy or powerful man. As a result, free women might choose concubinage in order to exercise some degree of autonomy, and poor women might choose concubinage over poverty, instability, and servitude.

Prayer

Bishop Thorlak, you who rejoice in perpetual peace, you embellished and made beautiful the sight of Christianity in Skálaholt with the making of your precepts, cutting away the unsightliness of people's vices. I ask you, Thorlak, cut with the scythe of your workings the thorns casting shadows in my unclear mind, that with a pure mind I may applaud your deeds at once, you who deserve praise by all and veneration.

Acknowledgments

I could not have written these stories without the kindness of so very many people.

In particular, I am grateful to Monsieur Adrien Wendling, of Sanctuaire du Mont Sainte-Odile, Archdiocese of Strasbourg, France, for the prayer to St. Odilia; Fr. Gregory Hallam, Dean at the Antiochian Orthodox Deanery of the United Kingdom and Ireland and priest at St. Aidan's Orthodox Church in Manchester, and his assistant priest, Fr. Emmanuel, for resources regarding St. Etheldreda; Aimée O'Connell, author, third-order Carmelite and founder of Autism Consecrated, for resources regarding St. Thorlak; Maggie Taylor, who shared her historical knowledge and insights; Mother Lois Farag, Ph.D., professor of Early Church History at Luther Seminary and Coptic Orthodox monastic, for her explanation of how the Roman legal system affected women debtors; and the servant of God Daniel for the prayer to St. John the Short.

I am also grateful to my friends Melissa DiSpaltro, Sarah Hodges, Michelle Mewhinney-Angel, Ann Pougas, and Tracy Thallas, who read the stories at various stages and alerted me to literary and historical blunders. Any blunders that remain are, of course, entirely my own fault.

I am grateful to my friend and editor, Summer Kinard, for her faith in this project and in me.

Finally, I am grateful to my husband, Alex. I couldn't have finished this book without his patience, insights, expert editing, and love.

Also From Park End Books

Available from ParkEndBooks.com

& wherever books are sold.

Accessible Church School: Incarnational Practices for Participating in God

Summer Kinard

Unlock faith formation for all learners with proven patterns.

The Grace of Being There: Single Mother Saints in Our Lives

Discover the grace of being there from women whose lives show you the God who meets every mother right where she is.

Become All Flame: Lent with African Saints

Fr. Deacon John R. Gresham, Jr.

Recovering the tradition of African Christian holy men and women from centuries-long neglect, Fr. Deacon John restores the sacredness of early African Christians to modern seekers.

That God's Works Might Be Revealed: Stories of Saints, Sickness, and Disabilities

By Charlotte Riggle

Be encouraged by the example of faithful people with disabilities whose sanctity changed their worlds.

Enter the worlds of 14 saints who lived holy lives with disabilities in these immersive stories. Featuring rarely-heard tales of St. Luca Casali, St. Finian Lobhar, St. Hervé, St. Etheldreda, St. Cenydd of Wales, St. Pimen the Much-Ailing, St. Theodore of Tobolsk, St. Hermann of Reichenau, St. Gerald of Aurillac, St. Angadrisma of Beauvais, St. John the Little, St. Nicholas of Myra, St. Odilia of Alsace, and St. Thorlak of Iceland, this volume will inspire Christians to see God's presence in the lives of people with disabilities.

www.ingramcontent.com/pod-product-compliance
Lightning Source LLC
Chambersburg PA
CBHW020048170426
43199CB00009B/206